The Worst Noel

The
Worst
Noel

HELLISH HOLIDAY TALES

HarperCollins*Publishers*

FIRST EDITION

Designed by Joseph Rutt

Printed on acid-free paper

Library of Congress Cataloging-in-Publication Data
The worst Noel : hellish holiday tales.—1st ed.
p. cm.
ISBN-10: 0-06-083811-6
ISBN-13: 978-0-06-083811-9
1. Horror tales, American. 2. Holidays—Fiction.

PS648.H6W67 2005
813'.0873808334—dc22
2005050229

06 07 08 09 10 ❖/RRD 10 9 8 7 6 5 4 3 2 1

CONTENTS

CHRISTMAS IN PARIS
Mike Albo

WE REALLY MUST GET TOGETHER
THIS YEAR
Marian Keyes

THE GIFT OF THE MAGI REDUX
Binnie Kirshenbaum

A FOREIGN COUNTRY
Mitchell Symons

THE JEW WHO COOKED A HAM
FOR CHRISTMAS
Neal Pollack

RUM BALLS
Roger Director

The Worst Noel

DONNER IS DEAD

Cynthia Kaplan

———— ◆ ————

A deer hit us. We were driving along, minding our own business when a deer jumped out of the woods, or maybe it jumped out of another car, who knows, and ran smack into us. We were driving north on Route 7, about five minutes out of Bennington, on our way to celebrate A Jew's Christmas in Vermont.

Christmas is jolly in Vermont. All the lights and the wreaths and the snow-tipped steeples. You can light candles every night for a year and shake groggers until Haman rises from the dead, but Hanukkah isn't fooling anyone. It's a diversionary tactic, kind of a "hey, over here" that Jewish parents employ to keep their children from feeling like those toys that get shipped out to the Island of Misfit Toys in *Rudolph, the Red-Nosed Reindeer*. Everyone claims that Hanukkah isn't meant to compete with the Christmas holiday. "It's a festival, it's a festival!" No one even knows when the hell it is. It changes every year. I'm not sure the *Farmers' Almanac* could predict it correctly.

Anyway, we didn't see it coming. All of a sudden, there was a very loud *thunk,* and then what seemed like a two-hundred-pound snowball exploded up and over the front windshield. My husband yelled, "What the fuck?" and I yelled, "Fuck!"

We pulled over to the shoulder and sat for a moment in silence, trying to make sense of what had just happened. It was a clear, bright night and very, very cold, maybe ten degrees; you could see for half a mile. There'd been nothing in the road. "I hope that was a deer," David said. "What else could it have been?" I asked. "I don't know," he said. "A person?"

David called the Bennington Police and then, with some difficulty because the door seemed able to open only about ten inches, he got out of the car and walked around the front. Through the windshield, which, thankfully, was still there, I saw him mouth "Holy shit." He squeezed back into the car and said that the driver's-side headlight was gone and the whole front left of the car was smashed in. The snowball effect we had experienced must have been the glass from the headlight shooting up like sparks in the dark. The driver's-side mirror was gone. David thought he saw some deer fur stuck to the ragged metal. Thank God.

There were police lights up ahead. A patrol car passed us by about two hundred yards, crossed the median, and came to a halt. The police were going to check on the deer first.

Here's what I don't understand: Why didn't Darwinism work for deer? Cars have been around for what, over one hundred years, right? Why haven't the stupidest deer died out? Why isn't the gene that tells a deer to cross a four-lane highway obsolete? Why aren't the smart deer at home in their beds making more smart deer?

What's wrong with deer, I ask you? Zebras have stripes, for God's sake, giraffes have long necks. The leopards that survive in snowy climes are *white*. Was this an accident? No! The white leopards outlived the orangey ones because they were harder to see. And they made more white leopards and now, now we have something called, yes, the s*now leopard.*

Where is the evolved deer? Haven't we waited long enough? They've certainly turned *tick-carrying* into a cottage industry. *That* didn't take long. Where is the deer that has a natural aversion to headlights? The deer who doesn't like the clickety-clacking noise his hoofs make on asphalt? Where is the deer that doesn't like the way it feels to lie dying in the middle of the road, wondering what the fuck just happened? Where is he? You know where? In the middle of the road wondering what the fuck just happened, that's where. And while we're asking, what's on the other side that's so important to see at eleven o'clock at night? Better woods?

———◆———

While we waited for the police, we discussed the fate of the deer. Was it dead? Was it mortally injured? Was there a driver's-side mirror protruding from its head, like an extra set of antlers? The police took so long with the deer that we imagined they must have found it alive and were either setting its legs in plaster of Paris or delivering the final death blow. No shots were fired, so perhaps they were wringing its neck.

Our five-year-old son woke up. Thankfully, his little sister slept on. She would not have been pleased to be sitting on the side of the road at eleven o'clock at night still strapped into her infernal five-point harness. John wanted to know why we'd stopped. Were we in Vermont? he asked. He has finally begun to grasp that Vermont is not just a 1960s faux Swiss chalet with orange shag carpeting and a sectional couch, but a whole land mass, with other houses and trees and people. We told him about the deer, making the distinction that the deer had hit us, not we it. If John had been a few years older and had had a bit of U.S. history under his belt, he might have said something impudent about how the deer were there first, like the Native Americans. In his youthful ignorance, however, he forgave the *deer,* proclaiming that it hadn't meant to hit us and "crack" our car, that it had been an "accident," and that the deer was probably sorry. Yes, I said. The deer was sorry. Very sorry.

When the police got to us, there were four of them, all without coats. They examined the car and made recommendations about how to proceed with our insurance company. In the fall and winter months, this must be their main activity—cleaning deer viscera off the highway and advising motorists on their reimbursement options. Of course, there was a hearty round of thanks that no one was hurt, not counting the deer. There have been more tragic outcomes, and we knew we were blessed. Our airbags had not even deployed. It was a Christmas miracle.

The policemen went back to their cars to write an accident report, and one of them returned about five minutes later with a copy for us. When he handed it to David through the window, he told us in a hushed voice to be careful when we got in and out of the left side of the car, because deer feces was splattered all over it. It's not uncommon, said the policeman.

Huh. So the deer took a crap on our car. I suppose this is some sort of natural phenomenon. The bowels releasing their contents in the midst of a trauma. I think I've heard that humans do this as well, in one of the final stages of the death process. But from the deer, it felt like an insult, a parting shot, revenge. *You killed me, so I shit on you.* How'd he do it so fast, though? He was going one way, we were going the other at, say, sixty-five miles an hour. It's not like we saw him mouthing "Fuck you" through the driver's-side window as he flipped past. How is it possible he clung to the car long enough to take a shit, and we hadn't seen him? It's like one of those mind-numbing algebra problems, the ones about the birds flying at different speeds over different distances and you have to figure out how the yellow-breasted pippledecker got to Cincinnati first.

We got up and skied the next day, driving our cracked, deer-fouled car to the mountain and back. After yelling, "Don't touch the car!" at the kids about forty times, David finally took it to a do-it-yourself car wash in Manchester. The day after Christmas, we returned to Manhattan at night in a blinding snowstorm, with one headlight and no driver's-side mirror, flouting Darwin.

———————

When we got home, I thought a great deal about the deer we'd killed. John thought about it, too. He had created a spectacular narrative of the accident, such as he knew it, editing and polishing it in order to present it at school during the first morning meeting after the break: "We were driving so so so fast, faster than all the cars, but not as fast as a cheetah. Cheetahs are not the fastest animals on earth. They are the fastest *land* animals. Then Santa was flying infinity high in the sky and his sleigh was going so so so fast. Then two deer fell off and fell on our car and SMASH. Just like this: SMASH! But they didn't do it on purpose. Why would they hit us on purpose? It was an accident." How the Santa thing got in there I've no idea. We may not be the most observant Jews, but we definitely draw the line at Santa. I also don't know where the second deer came from. Very grassy knoll.

I couldn't get over the fact that we'd killed something as large as a deer. Not that we kill a lot of small animals. Well, once, driving home from college in a rainstorm, I hit a duck. And we do kill a good number of flies. It is something of an alternate sport in Vermont, like snowshoeing. During the winter months the flies that live in ski houses become cryogenically paralyzed. When we show up and turn on the heat, they sort of half revive and flop listlessly around the white sand–sprayed ceiling like stoned beach bums. David walks around with the flyswatter and John follows with a 1975 Electrolux. I suppose if I were a true animal activist, I would not make a distinction between the value of the life of a deer and that of a fly, but I'm not.

Really, what is it those deer are thinking about when they are standing like statues by the side of the road, ready to spring forward to their deaths? What's on their minds? Why can't they get with the program? Hey, if you don't like the cars, get out of New England. I'm not particularly fond of research except as a tool of procrastination, but I felt I needed to know why deer were so obtuse. There must be some fundamental, scientific basis for their inability to adapt to the industrial age. I went to the library, and let me tell you, there's a *dearth* of literature on the subject. It's pathetic. In the *Eye Wonder* series, of which we are particularly fond, the deer rate a quarter of a page in the book dedicated to *the forest.* Our only other option was the book version of Disney's *Bambi,* not the most reliable source of serious information. Then it came to me—*Bambi. Not* the Disney version but the original 1928 novel by Felix Salten. I read it in seventh-grade English and I remember being deeply moved, deeply. So I got it out of my library and spent an afternoon rereading it.

Now, I'm sure the story of Bambi is familiar to most. Bambi is a deer born in a forest glade on a warm summer day. He becomes friends with most of the other forest animals—various birds, squirrels, etc.—and a few other deer. Unlike the animated movie, however, this *Bambi* was not meant for small children. I'm not sure it was really meant for *any* children. The deer are at the mercy of the hunter, whom they refer to as Him, and first Bambi's mother and then many of his friends are shot and killed. Around Christmas, with everyone being on vacation and all, there is something of an all-forest massacre.

What strikes me most about the novel now is how stupid the deer appear to be. Their conversation is inane, they seem to be ruled entirely by a mixture of confusing urges, and they are unable to identify distinct emotions or to separate them from their polar opposites. They are both terrified and titillated at the same time. They either stand frozen or run completely amok. Their sense of smell is sharp, but their memories are vague. They wander off mid-conversation.

The words "I don't understand" follow their every utterance, action, or emotion. They're dumb as posts. All the other animals in the forest remark upon their stupidity. Even the squirrels.

Furthermore, their fathers neither live with them nor acknowledge their paternity. Bambi does not know that the old stag who eventually saves his life is his father until the stag is on his own deathbed. As soon as Bambi is able to fend for himself, his mother begins disappearing for days, even weeks at a time, probably off following the stags around, hoping for a little action. After what seems like a monthslong absence, she returns for a visit and is killed while leading Bambi across a field. Bambi's cousin, Gobo, who has always been weaker than his peers, collapses while trying to escape a hunting expedition and is rescued by the hunter himself, taken home, and made a domestic pet. When he is released into the wild again, he displays no memory of previous horrors. He spends his days bragging about the food that appeared regularly in his little deer dish and the pleasures of life among the fraternity of farm animals and dogs. One day he prances out into the open meadow and is promptly shot to death.

Finally, of all things, Bambi falls in love with Faline, Gobo's sister. Faline is Bambi's first cousin. Hmm. Perhaps this is why natural selection has failed with deer. Instead of marrying up, they reproduce with their own equally stupid relatives, honing their genetic material to a half a helix or something and creating generations upon generations of car-chasing dolts who seem particularly fond of leading their families and friends across four-lane highways. If lemmings are the People's Temple of the animal kingdom ("Drink the Kool-Aid, drink the Kool-Aid"), deer are the Heaven's Gate: *It's okay. You just need some Nikes and a plastic bag and you're good to go.* Sure, I've dashed across a busy city street against the light, but I always, *always* look both ways and never, *ever* do it with my kids. All things being equal, although no things really are, deer seem to have gotten themselves into a dangerous groove. I don't know what it will take to get them out of it. Higher fences? Stricter penalties? Genetic counseling?

———————

Don't get me wrong. I have a deep and abiding esteem for the members of the animal kingdom. That they have survived at all in a world populated by the cruelest of creatures, i.e., Man, is miraculous. I feel neither good nor superior about the death of that deer. It was tragic, and what's more, killing an animal from the relative safety of my station wagon makes me feel like a Republican, which I do not like *at all.* And in fact, I, myself, do stupid things all the time. Why, just last week I drove home from Vermont with my family in a blinding snowstorm with one headlight and no driver's-side mirror. I'm lucky to be alive.

BLUE CHRISTMAS: THE TOUR

John Marchese

———•———

*I*t wasn't until I went down into the jungle room of Elvis's Graceland mansion that I realized how lucky Lisa Marie was that her daddy died so young. She never had to bring a boyfriend home to meet him at Christmastime.

This probably shouldn't be the train of thought a person rides while taking the Graceland tour. I suppose that most people who pony up twenty-seven dollars to walk through the house have a more reverential view of the King. But it was two days till Christmas and I was in Memphis with my fiancée and we were driving southwest from New York as slowly as possible, with as many stops as were feasible, because our ultimate destination was her hometown in Texas. It was time for me to meet her family. This was an appointment that I could no longer avoid, but I could take my time getting there.

Meeting the family of my significant other is a rite of passage that I have made a few too many times. The great-to-meet-you, I've-heard-a-lot-about-you, no-I've-never-been-to-(city/state)-before routine is as predictable and dull as . . . well, a Christmas pageant. Which is fitting, since for me it has always seemed to happen at Christmas, a holiday that, according to statistics I've seen, makes many people cranky and depressed. I am one of those people. Consequently, in meet-the-family performances past, my lines have often become a "Do-you-have-any-Scotch? I-think-I'll-turn-in-early, Honey-can-we-go-home-*today*?" routine.

Over the years, as I passed from girlfriend to girlfriend, every few Christmases I would collect a new package of not-really-relatives wrapped, invariably, in red-and-green sweaters. There were the Plumbers of Philadelphia. It wasn't their name but the family profession, and father and brothers spent the holy holiday looking at me funny and wondering why I didn't work for a living. There were the Professors of Pittsburgh, who were smart and funny and who maintained an enviably rigid cocktail-hour schedule, but who sometimes seemed to be enacting their own little-theater revival of *Who's Afraid of Virginia Woolf?* Over the years, as the Christmas meet-and-greets piled up, I actually began to miss one otherwise thankfully lost girlfriend from my early twenties. Her one redeeming quality was that she was an orphan.

Dixie, as I will call my fiancée, had told me tales of her family that made it seem to defy easy categorization. On an alphabetized spectrum of familial examples, I had the notion that her clan would be somewhere between Addams and von Trapp, perhaps tending toward the family named Manson. She thought they were a hoot.

First off, they were Texan, which calls off all bets on behavior. Second, they were what is called *blended,* with a stepmother and stepsister and stepbrother and other extended steps. Third, they were born again, which I took to mean that they would greet me at the front door, get a whiff of my Roman Catholic heathenism, and run panting for the Bible.

Where I came from, Catholics took Christmas as a kind of eating festival. There wasn't much actual religion involved. Going to church on Christmas was required, of course. For lots of people it was the only day out of 365 that they went to church. Because of the overflow this caused, the rules of attendance were loosened and my family migrated to a late-night time slot—Midnight Mass. When I was a kid this seemed exciting, staying up late and getting a little high on the incense. Later, I realized that the adults preferred Midnight Mass because it allowed everyone to sleep late the next morning, and on this one day, church could be experienced after a nice meal and a few drinks. (Though in the case of my grandfather and uncle, only a sunrise service would preclude a few preparatory drinks, and probably not even then.)

Contrary to this, just after we crossed the Mississippi River out of Memphis, Dixie warned me that her father and stepmother might ask us to go to church *a few times*. Also, they did not drink. That seemed about the deadliest combination of habits that I could conceive: dry serial churchgoing. I pictured a grueling day of sober worship, like the Salvation Army scenes in *Guys and Dolls*. I thought of getting us into a minor, though time-consuming, auto accident somewhere around Little Rock.

But I didn't. It would only have delayed the inevitable. Newton might have said it: Bodies in motion toward meeting parents tend to remain in motion, no matter how many times those bodies try to postpone things by stopping at Stuckey's. By the same unfair and perverse laws, it was axiomatic that we would get to the parents' driveway, leave the car, and ring their doorbell.

"Well, hi therrrrrre. It's so good to finally meet youuuuuuuu. We've all been just so lookin' forward to this."

Dixie's stepmother, Miriam, told me I should call her Mi-Mi, because that's what all the grandchildren did when they were first learning to talk. Mi-Mi opened the door into what might have been a very nice Texas ranch house, except it looked like a Christmas bomb had gone off inside. Wreaths and ribbons and ornaments and garland and figurines filled the place. It was what an elf must see in his fevered dreams. A Christmas song was on the stereo. Lights twinkled. I got a whiff of gingerbread. At any moment, I expected Andy Williams to walk out of the kitchen.

Instead, out came Pee-Pee, which, of course, is not

Dixie's father's real name but what the grandchildren used to call him until they learned the unfortunate implications. I could call him Bob, he told me, which is what I did immediately, naturally. But I still can't quite think of him as anything but Pee-Pee. He was a big-bellied guy who seemed to reside on the opposite side of the land of enthusiasm from Mi-Mi, thank God. He wanted reports about our trip, and I could tell that he wouldn't be bored if I analyzed the variations in our gas mileage between the mountain and plains states. He'd been a bookkeeper.

"I've been to New York and all," Pee-Pee reported. "It's a great town, but I don't know how anyone could live there all the time. I mean, you can't even cross the street without just about gettin' killed. It's like that *Midnight Cowboy* movie." Dixie then pinched me in the back, and before I could ask her why, her father began his impersonation of Dustin Hoffman as Ratso Rizzo crossing a deadly Manhattan street.

"Ahhhhmmmm walkin' hairrrrr," Pee-Pee called out. "Ahhhhmmm walkin' hairrrrr."

I hadn't seen *Midnight Cowboy* in a while, but I was pretty certain that Ratso didn't have a thick Texas accent. I smiled at Pee-Pee with a big grin of wonderment and tried to decide whether I should at least compliment him on capturing Dustin Hoffman's feral intensity. But Mi-Mi broke things up.

"Who wants punch? Yawl gotta try my Christmas punch. It's wuuuuunderful." She virtually skipped into the kitchen.

Dixie pinched me again and whispered, "*Wuuuunderful* is her favorite word. She was a cheerleader."

I'd been briefed ahead of time by Dixie on the basic facts. I knew that Mi-Mi and Pee-Pee had gone through recovery for various things, and had been clean and sober for years, which was fine with me. But did that mean I had to drink the punch? There was a big vat of the goopy stuff. It contained colors that I don't think occur in nature. There were big chunks of melting sherbet floating around in the bowl. Mi-Mi passed around Christmas mugs that looked homemade. Since she and Pee-Pee had retired early (he had been a smart bookkeeper), Mi-Mi was discovering her creative, arty-crafty side. It wouldn't have surprised me if she'd crocheted me a cup right that minute. I accepted a mug full of punch, took a sip, and thought I might fall into diabetic shock.

"Wonderful indeed," I said. Dixie pinched me again.

Our wonderful punch sipping and small talk went on quite longer than I expected. We'd actually shown up on time, and it was a hidebound family tradition among Dixie's people to be incredibly late. Sipping her odd-colored punch, Mi-Mi said, "Don't you just lovvvvve the holidays?" and then repeated it again in about nine slightly different ways. Finally, Dixie's sister, Suzie, made it—only forty-five minutes behind schedule—dragging her daughter, Hannah, and a Pekingese named Fluffy, who was part of a cavalcade of Christmas presents for Hannah that included every American Girl doll ever produced and some that had never made it out of prototype.

Hannah was a great distraction, and Fluffy was even better because they took Mi-Mi away from our punch circle and into the living room full of pine scent and presents. Pee-Pee and Dixie and Suzie and I discussed the possibility that Suzie's husband, Bill, would actually make it for dinner. He sold things to convenience stores and drove around Texas for at least sixteen hours every day of the week, keeping up with his nonstop supply requirements. Dixie had taken to calling him Sasquatch, because whenever she visited her sister, Bill was often just a vague, lumbering shadow that passed through the house at odd hours. Suzie said she was sure he would make it for dinner, but that he'd better not fall asleep at the table, as he had done last year.

Then we heard Mi-Mi shouting in the other room. "Stop staring at me! Stop staring at me!"

"Hannah," Suzie called. "Stop staring at Grandma."

"It wasn't her," Mi-Mi said, rushing into the kitchen and pouring herself a soothing punch. "It was that dog. That dog was staring at me!"

Mi-Mi's sweater had so many shiny green and red beads sewn in the shape of a Christmas tree that a normal dog could easily have become transfixed. Fluffy wasn't being bad; he was probably hypnotized. Pee-Pee took Fluffy to the garage for a time-out. Hannah started to cry. Mi-Mi was sweating a little and seemed to be vibrating. Someone that tightly strung needed something besides neon sherbet in her punch.

Dixie and I had taken Hannah to see Fluffy in the garage when Dixie's stepbrother, Trey-Trey, arrived. He was a sallow and thinner version of his father, and when I got close enough to shake his hand, I developed a notion of why he was late. From the smell, I guessed that Trey-Trey had offered a Rastafarian reggae band a ride to their gig. Trey-Trey was in his mid-thirties and drove for a living.

"You still working for Dominos?" Dixie asked her stepbrother.

"Nah, that was two jobs ago," he told her. "I was workin' as a host at TGI Friday's, but that ended a few weeks ago."

"What happened?"

"Ah, you know how things are in big corporations. It's all just politics."

There wasn't time to analyze the Machiavellian nature of surviving in the restaurant jungle that is TGI Friday's because Dixie and Trey-Trey's grandfather showed up right then. Of course, his name was Paw-Paw.

Paw-Paw was wearing a bright white turtleneck and a well-cut soft-leather aviator jacket. He looked like the most prosperous man in that part of Texas, though I knew he was not. On his arm was Grace, a little woman with a slight stoop. (How long would it be before they compounded her name?) Grace was Paw-Paw's new girlfriend. They'd met in the assisted-living facility where he'd gone after his wife died. Paw-Paw had waited a respectable couple of weeks before replacing his wife of sixty years.

Grace and Paw-Paw went into the house, got their punch, and headed for a sofa, where they nuzzled like teenagers. I saw Mi-Mi looking at her father and his new girlfriend and thought that at any minute her head might just start spinning around. I tried very hard not to stare.

It seemed that dinner could begin any time now, it being almost two hours past the scheduled time. But still no Sasquatch spotting, and we were waiting on the Dickeys. That was Dixie's stepsister and her new husband, Willie, whom the family thought had lots of good qualities compared with her first two husbands. Willie drove a bigger truck than numbers one and two, carried a bigger knife on his belt, and kept a steady job. The biggest drawback was that marrying him meant becoming Vicki Dickey, but everyone was adjusting.

They finally arrived—separately. It turned out that the Dickeys had managed to be individually late. "I ain't seen you all day," Willie said to Vicki. "Gimme a kiss." She pecked at him, and he pulled her around and said, "I mean a *real* kiss, woman," and proceeded to go at her with a fervor that made me blush. Across the room, Paw-Paw started to whistle and applaud.

And so, without Sasquatch, we sat down to dine.

Through dinner, I kept flashing back to Graceland and how it might have been for Lisa Marie to bring her latest beau home for a Yuletide bacon-and–peanut-butter sandwich with Dad. Would the table chatter have been any better than Paw-Paw outlining his plans for his impending marriage to, and honeymoon with, Grace? Would Priscilla, if she'd stayed with Elvis, have been able, as Mi-Mi was, to make a totally dry turkey that seemed to come with macramé crust?

People think that Tolstoy said, "All happy families are boring in the same way." But he just said, "Happy families are all alike." Happy or not, all families—crazy or corny, dignified or dysfunctional—are unique. And oddly, in that way they're all the same. It's what makes them both unendurable and sustaining at the same time. Mi-Mi was trying to force-feed me her special green Jell-O with marshmallows (molded into a Santa shape). I took a sip of sparkling cider and realized that this family was fine with me. As weird as they all seemed now, a day would come soon when they'd be as warm and dull as a piece of toast. I would marry Dixie and stay with her forever. That way, I would never have to meet another new family, especially during the crankiest time of the year.

After dinner we all stood in the kitchen around a big sheet cake that said JESUS in red frosting and was decked out with birthday candles. Pee-Pee lit the candles, asked us to join hands, and started us in singing "Happy Birthday" to Jesus. As it happened, I was standing between Trey-Trey and Willie Dickey, and the three of us holding hands must have looked like the true definition of discomfort.

"Happy Birthday, dear Jeeesuuuus," we sang. "Happy Birthday to you." Dixie couldn't help herself, and as the song finished, she added, "And many morrrrrre." Sasquatch showed up then, fixed himself a cold plate, and fell asleep in front of the fireplace. We all played a present-swapping game and ate more sugar. I felt sick and content. Another Christmas had come and gone. Bless us one and all.

We were getting ready to leave when Mi-Mi presented me with her handmade "Thankfulness Book" and ordered me to write in it what I was most thankful for on this holiday. The effect of having to write something on cue made my mind a desolate tundra, devoid of thoughts, frozen.

"It should be easy for you," Mi-Mi said, hovering. "You're a writer." She was staring at me. *That woman was staring at me!*

I shook myself to attention, and the first thankful thought came to me: *That Christmas comes but once a year.* I had to pull away my writing hand, Dr. Strangelove–fashion, to keep from putting that into Mi-Mi's arty-crafty little book.

Instead, I set the pen down on the thick colored paper and wrote, "Getting to know my new family. Merry Christmas."

EIGHT

Amy Krouse Rosenthal

———◆———

1.

There was the Christmas when I was growing up where we went to my cousin Andy's in-laws' house. We were greeted at the door by a warm and gracious, albeit unfamiliar, matriarch. After being motioned inside and handing over our coats, we gathered in the living room with the other also unfamiliar guests. We half chitchatted, half waited for our cousin and his family to appear. The dialogue had to have been stilted and off-kilter, not unlike the odd feeling of trying to make sense of a conversation when you're catching only every third word. Twenty minutes later, and still no cousin. Could he really be tied up this long with guests in another room? We finally—because we are smart that way—realized that we were not at our cousin's in-laws' house at all. *Oh, you want the Cairo family! You want the house next door! We wondered who you were, too! Oh well, nice to meet you, folks! Take care! Merry Christmas!*

There was the Christmas not too long ago when I went head to head with a virus that was clearly not on holiday. This nasty and persistent little bug first had its way with my insides. That was followed by a few hours of commercial-free vomiting. Next came the passing out in the bathtub trick, where I came to only after flooding the bathroom and the entire bedroom. Then I pretended I was fine (fooling exactly zero people), deteriorated to the point of hallucinations, and ultimately ended up in the hospital.

Those were weird and unfortunate Christmases, respectively. But the *worst* Christmas I ever had was, hands down, the Christmas I found out I wasn't Christian.

2.

I was eight. I knew I was Jewish on some level. I knew I wasn't Christian like other people were Christian. But I thought I was some sort of you-got-Judaism-on-my-Christianity/no-you-got-Christianity-on-my-Judaism amalgam. See, there's Orthodox Jews, Conservative Jews, Reformed Jews, and Children-of-the-'70s Jews. All the Jewish kids I grew up with were pretty much a member of that last sect. I don't say it like *oh, everyone was doing it* as a way to make it sound more acceptable. I say it because in retrospect I find it interesting when you look at it in its historical context, how the pendulum/Jewish households swung after World War II. There were a great many little Jewish boys and girls all over the country who had trees in their living rooms, stockings on their mantels, and chocolate chip cookies for Santa on the table.

3.

This stocking footnote: My grandmother's friend Gladys knit one for each of us four children. They were red and happy looking, with spots of soft white fur and our names along the top. They were a treasure, and they represented everything that was merry about Christmas.

Shortly after meeting my husband, another child of the '70s, I discovered that he also had his very own "Gladys stocking." Turns out that Jason's grandmother was friendly with the queen knitter as well. This certainly goes back to the point about the prevalence of the Christmas spirit across the faiths in my generation, but it's also just a nice bit of serendipity, wouldn't you say?

4.

The year 1973 was when my parents agreed it was time to pack up the ornaments and bring out the Judaism. Up until then, our Jewish rituals consisted of Chinese food for dinner every Sunday night, being scolded in Yidlish (half English, half Yiddish, as in, *Oy, vay iz mir, turn off* The Brady Bunch *and clean up this mess),* and one full-fledged holiday—Passover at my aunt Barbara and uncle Henry's. We had joined our first temple earlier that year—I was starting Sunday school—and it was the rabbi who suggested to my folks that having a Christmas tree might be, you know, a tad conflicting for a Jewish child. Interestingly, all of our ornaments were hand-me-downs from another Jewish family, good friends of my parents whose kids were a few years older than us, and they had come to this exact same Christmas/Hanukkah crossroad (no pun intended, but I do rather like it) a few years before.

I suppose then that my worst Christmas was technically my first non-Christmas. All my prior Christmases, as best as I can remember, were pretty white, bright, and excellent. We went from Christmas morning to Christmas mourning.

5.

Looking back on this time, I would say that I remember Christmas feeling very big, and Hanukkah feeling very small. It was as if the day after Thanksgiving someone flipped a switch and Christmas was "on" everywhere. People's houses were magnificently decorated. (*Where did all those lights come from? Who's making them blink on and off like that? How'd they get that big plastic Santa on the roof?*) Mothers and daughters wore red-and-green matching knit sweaters. *Frosty* and *Charlie Brown* and *Miracle on 34th Street* came back from wherever they had been hibernating and permeated the tube. Talk of stocking stuffers and gifts was omnipresent. Everyone knew on Tuesday that there were 16 shopping days left, and then everyone agreed on Wednesday that there were 15 days left. Candy canes were everywhere in such abundance—at school, at stores, at the car wash—that you could eat one without your mom counting it as dessert, almost like we were obligated to help consume them. And so in contrast to all this, Hanukkah felt like a P.S. It also felt distinctly foreign and insular, like a science experiment with confusing instructions that you tried to figure out all by yourself in the basement.

6.

That first Hanukkah may not have entered with a bang, but it did enter with a bush—the never-popular Hanukkah bush. (My sister recalls it this way: "Man, that thing was cheap." Not surprisingly, my parents didn't bother with the stout plastic shrubbery after that first year.) Digging deep into my memory, I see some fuzzy, halfhearted dreidel-playing—that really never really caught on, either. However, those coin chocolates wrapped in pinched gold foil—that was something we could get excited about. My mom serenaded us with "Herman the Hanukkah Candle," sung to the tune of "Rudolph, the Red-Nosed Reindeer." Where she learned this, I have no idea. But it was cute and sweet, in a sad, consolation-prize kind of way.

What was truly special about Hanukkah—aside from the fact that as long as you ended it with an *h* and inserted a *k* or two in there, you could pretty much spell it any way you wanted—was the lighting of the menorah. Unlike the Hanukkah bush, unlike Herman T.H.C., the menorah was all ours. It wasn't borrowed or adapted or a Jewish version of a Christian something. It would be years before I completely understood the hows and whys of Hanukkah, but I did understand, from the very first candle on that very first night, that it was beautiful and it made us quiet and that it was something I rightfully and naturally belonged to.

7.

As a Jewish adult living in a Christian world, I find that most people generally assume everyone celebrates Christmas. And that's okay. We get to wade in some of the joy and jingle without having to do any of the heavy lifting. "Merry Christmas!" a clerk will say as I leave a store. "Merry Christmas to you, too!" I'll say, like I'm one with humanity. I know people mean it more in a polite way—more akin to "Have a good weekend!" than "Happy birth of Jesus!"—so I typically just go along with it. On the rare occasion where I do say, "Well, actually, I'm Jewish, so I don't celebrate Christmas, I celebrate Hanukkah," there's this awkward apologizing and backtracking. "Have a great New Year," we'll agree, and that's always a nice peace offering.

(It does happen, and not infrequently, I should say, that someone who knows I'm Jewish will be confused about how I, as a Jewish person, operate in the month of December. If I had a dime for every time someone said to me, "I know you're Jewish, but you still, like, celebrate Christmas, right?" I would be set for life in Hanukkah gelt.)

8.

It's 2005. I have a family of my own. Our youngest child just turned eight. Our kids have never had a Christmas, good or bad.

We have Shabbat dinner every Friday, and we say the prayers. In addition to Passover and the high holidays, we've added Purim, Sukkoth, and Simchat Torah to our holiday shindig repertoire. Our oldest child is studying for his Bar Mitzvah. Pre-marriage, I backpacked through Israel, and my folks have traveled there twice in the last few years. Our journey, our transformation, is by no means unique—it is true for so many of the Jewish families I know in all corners of the country.

While Jason and I still cherish our merry pair of Gladys stockings, the box we unpack every December contains not ornaments but a collection of menorahs our kids have made over the years. Hanukkah no longer feels small to me. It feels big—big, bright, good, and full of chocolate.

THAT'S JUST ABOUT *ENOUGH* FIGGY PUDDING, ACTUALLY

Catherine Newman

*Y*ou can't always put your finger on it, can you? What it is exactly that makes the holidays feel like one big sucked-sharp candy cane poking into your eye? I mean, if one of those little blinking bulbs shorts out and your Tannenbaum goes up in flames, setting fire first to the paisley drapes and then to the exposed beams, and finally burning your whole house to the ground while you stand outside in the sleet in your long underwear, watching—well, you can certainly put your finger on *that*. Or maybe the repo man comes to your door dressed up as Santa Claus and he's all, *Ho ho ho, give me the keys to the Honda.* That always sucks. Or it's 1877 in Minnesota, and you're Pa Ingalls, harebrained prairie patriarch, shivering in a snow cave while the blizzard rages outside, and after you've kept yourself alive for three days on Christmas candy and oyster crackers, it turns out you're not even fifty yards from the very sod house on the banks of Plum Creek where your wife and three daughters are tatting their lace! Now, *there's* a good story about a bad Christmas.

But sometimes nothing happens—really, there's an almost otherworldly absence of anything happening, and the kids don't even wake up barfing all over their holiday pajamas—but each irritating non-thing is like a little Yuletide ant under your shirt until you're just clawing at your own skin and glugging Benadryl from the bottle.

Maybe it starts with the tree. Wouldn't it be fun to go to one of those pick-your-own Christmas tree farms? No. It wouldn't. But since you'll go anyway, why don't you run ahead and tip the teenagers five dollars to *not* offer your husband a saw to cut the tree down himself? Because even though Michael, my own man-person, is someone who'll happily tie on an apron before getting down on his hands and knees to scrub the crusty floor of the oven, and even though he can stand comfortably in the feminine hygiene aisle trying to remember if I said "Super" or "Super Plus"— as soon as he sees a forest and a saw, his Inner Manliness is going to demand that he wrangle some poor tree into submission. The teenagers might as well ask, "Hey, do you want the saw to cut it down yourself? Or would you prefer that we staple the word *pussy* to your back and cut it down for you?" And whatever it is that you picture—maybe his standing in a dry sort of way and moving his arm back and forth like one of those windmill lawn-ornament lumberjacks until the whole tree snaps unequivocally over—it's nothing like that.

What it's like is Michael kneeling in the mud and melty snow, ducking under the low branches that are welting up the back of his neck and depositing sap into his hair, while he hacks at the place he imagines the trunk might be. Don't forget helpful me—"It's a saw, honey, not an *axe*"—or Michael's expleting of the words *shit* and then *fuck* when the tree starts to bend one way and then teeters sideways before, at the last second, crashing down over his kneeling back. You can "Good King Wenceslas" all you want in the car driving home—nobody's going to join in.

Then come the inconsequential holiday misunderstandings. "Hey," I say to Michael, when we're warm and dry again. "Would you mind getting the tree skirt down for me?" "Sure," he says, and disappears into the attic. Meanwhile Ben, who is five, has plunked himself down in front of the tree stand, elbows on the ground, chin on his fists. He lies there unblinking for five or so minutes before I say, "What's up, Kittycat?" "Well," he says, "you said the tree was thirsty, and I'm waiting to see if it's going to drink." I picture what he's picturing—some throated sort of hole opening up in the trunk and gulping water—and am suddenly reminded of my mother saying I needed to wear cotton underpants so my vagina could "breathe." I used to sit in my second-grade classroom, terrified that everyone would hear it choking and gasping for air under my nylon tights. (Of course, decades later, in an Ashtanga yoga class, it did once sigh audibly. But I don't think this is what my mom had in mind.)

We're still in front of the tree, Ben and I, waiting for it to drink, when Michael returns. "I couldn't find it in any of the clothes bins," he says. "Is it a skirt that's *shaped* like a Christmas tree? Or does it just have a tree *pattern* on it? To tell you the truth, I can't even remember your wearing it."

Oy vey.

Next comes an excursion to the Christmas Loft Holiday Emporium, where Ben is hoping to purchase an Advent calendar. I have promised to make him one—complete with many liftable flaps and many cute pictures of cute animals opening cute presents—but Ben wants a "real one." And by "real" he means, of course, *shrink-wrapped*. "A real Advent calendar?" he muses in the car, like the little half-Jew expert he is. "An actual one? I think you need to, you know, tear it open or rip it out of some sort of a package." He pantomimes this rending with his fingers. Yes, of course. We're not in a cave eking out our existence on oyster crackers, for God's sake! It's modern-day America. If it's worth having, it's worth wrapping in plastic. Our lives are like *The Velveteen Rabbit,* only "real" and "fake" have been switched around in some horrible existential inversion. "What?" Ben says. "What did you say?" And I say, "Oh, nothing. I guess I was just thinking aloud."

What can a person really say about the Christmas Loft Holiday Emporium? It's just like you knew it was going to be: the rooms are so velvety and hushed and dark, it's as if you're in a museum of the world's most faceted jewels, only what there is to see is as earnest and pointless and frightening as a dog's fancy sweater. Walls of complicated neo-heirloom ornaments. (I'm tempted to buy one for Michael with the words "Dear Husband" glitter-embossed on a plaid ceramic necktie.) A heavy, expensive snow globe in which Frosty's snow head seems to have come loose and now wafts around decapitatedly with the glitter and flakes. Round-mouthed figurines, like so many little caroling versions of Munch's *The Scream*. Surrounded by the holiday fumes—a cross between Pine-Sol, Atomic Fireballs, and clove cigarettes—and "White Christmas" leaking from the vents like so much toxic gas, murmured, it seems, by robots, Ben is in heaven.

He stops to ooh and ah over each fur-trimmed velvet stocking and glass candy cane and dreidel ornament (don't even talk to me about the dreidel ornaments) until, eventually, we arrive at the sanctum sanctorum of the entire complex: the Room of the Miniature Villages. It is so beautiful to him that Ben actually gasps, says "Mama!" and takes my hand. Awe creates a nearly visible glow around the boy, though the space itself is dark, lit only by miniature streetlights and the glowing windows of the miniature Alpine chalets. I have to hold Ben up so he can admire the paths paved with Starlight Mints, the shimmery-shammery polyester snowbanks, the tiny skaters scratching their endless figure eights onto a magnetized plastic pond. "We should write a book about this," Ben breathes. "About a kid who shrinks down and lives in this beautiful eentsy village, right here. Isn't that a good idea?" This produces in me a distinct and immediate *ka-ching* feeling, complete with dollar signs in my eyeballs—That *is* a good idea!—only in the book *I'd* want to write, the little boy would walk through all the miniature houses, and instead of holiday roasts and cheer, there would just be lots of wires and battery packs and tags that said "Made in Korea" and "$79.99." I don't think this is the kind of enchanted story Ben has in mind.

On our way out of the Emporium, plastic-wrapped calendar in hand, I am molested by a larger-than-life singing electronic Santa Claus. It chortles merrily, then swats at my ass with its white-gloved hand. Ben tosses a frightened glance over his shoulder before uttering the words of the enlightened: "There are probably some kids, maybe some really *little* kids, who think that's really the *real* Santa Claus? But it's not!" When I don't say anything, he adds, "Right?" and I say, "Right!" Though all I can think of is last summer's Teddy Bear Rally on the town common, where Ben—after being roughly embraced by a plush-costumed entertainer—asked, "Was that a *real* pretend teddy bear?" And I had to say, from the very heart of semantic uncertainty, "I'm not sure."

But Santa Claus. Here we arrive at the jolly hub of my holiday ennui. Because there's no way out but *through*, if you know what I'm saying. Who wants to be the cynical jerk who refuses a child the pleasure of mystery and magic?

Like, "Come on, Ben, climb back into your gray overalls so we can go wait in the bread line again." A child must believe! Which is fine when they're little, really, and the details of improbability are lost on them. *Amazing Saint Nick! Flies around with flying reindeer and knows you want a Dr Pepper Bonne Bell Lip Smacker!* But now Ben is a person grazing at the smorgasbord of logic—and Santa just doesn't fit in with the sequence of numbers and "that's why they're called *under*wear." Like one evening, we're reading an old book called *The Christmas Whale,* about the year the reindeer are down with the flu and Santa leaves the North Pole on whaleback, with stacks of gifts he unloads at various ports around the world. Something about this representation of a trip across the enormous globe sets Ben's gears to spinning.

"Wait," Ben says, and chops his hand through the air in a gesture that means *wait.* "How many kids are there in the whole world?"

"There are about six billion people," I say. "Maybe a quarter of those are kids—so maybe a billion and a half kids altogether. Picture grains of sand filling up a swimming pool."

Ben sucks his thumb thoughtfully. "And is that more than the number of seconds in the whole night?"

"Yes." I suddenly picture Santa biting into three billion oatmeal cookies in ten hours, gulping eight billion ounces of room-temperature milk. No wonder he's so freaking fat.

"I know the part about the whale is a pretend story? But

the real Santa has time to bring each child a present, all in one night?" Ben is chewing his cuticles now.

Two million chimney trips per second; Donner and Blitzen snorting diet pills and crank.

"Some families might have lots and lots of kids, so there are actually fewer stops," I offer, lamely.

"Maybe," Ben says. "But aren't some kids Jewish and also other religions, like the kids who celebrate solstice and Drama Don?"

"Ramadan," I say, and "Yes."

"Well, does Santa bring gifts to those kids?"

"I guess not," I say, "not if they don't celebrate Christmas." *Because Santa is a bigot.*

"Yes, but how does he know?" There is no way around Ben's reasonableness.

His Dobermans sniff them out.

"He's magic," I say. "He just knows."

"I don't think so." Ben sucks his thumb thoughtfully for a while. "I think he looks in your window, and if he sees a menorah—well, not just a menorah, like ours, but a menorah and no stockings or tree"—or *ham*—"then he flies away to the next house."

Unbidden, a pornographic Norman Rockwell painting pops into my mind: a jolly Santa face peering into the holly-trimmed window of a bedroom where a naked couple is nakedly coupling. A naked *Jewish* couple, maybe with a framed Chagall print hanging above their bed.

Who knew Santa was a peeping anti-Semite?

And not only that, but a *proliferating* peeping anti-Semite. Here he is at Sears, with a sweating beard and a Burger King bag crumpled under his chair! There he is next door at Penney's, his beard more yellow than white, a Dunkin' Donuts bag crumpled under his chair! And there he is at the town holiday parade, grunting, "Sorry, kid," before leaping onto the hayride ahead of Ben and galloping away on the last ride of the evening. *Ho ho ho. Fuck you.*

"And I guess," Ben continues, "when he looks in your window, that's how he figures out if you've been good or not." I can't tell if the peeper/stalker theory is more or less creepy than the concept of omniscience. (I imagine Santa borrowing God's yellow legal pad scrawled with holy notes about the world's children: "Stuck own tongue in outlet," "Bludgeoned sister with Pooh slipper.") Judging from Ben's pulled-together eyebrows, I'm guessing *more creepy.* I tell him that all kids are good and Santa knows it, and Ben relaxes enough to reminisce about the fiberglass reindeer he saw pooping out real pretend poops.

Until Christmas Day. That morning, Ben plucks thing after thing from his stocking, and he is as gracious and lovely as those *Little House on the Prairie* daughters, with their bright tin cups and one copper penny each. ("Oh Pa, you didn't!") "Scotch tape!" he cries. "Band-Aids!" "Embroidery thread!" Ben is surrounded by his loot. "Santa really *did* know what I wanted!" And then he reaches to the near-bottom of my old woolen sock and pulls out the snow globe. We have painstakingly cut out and inserted into this snow globe a photo from our last vacation, of Ben smiling into the sun in his blue-hibiscus swimsuit. Ben shakes the globe appreciatively, watches all the flakes drift down, then squints inside and freezes at the sight of himself. "Oh my God," he says, and his mouth drops open in horror. "Santa followed us to Mexico."

BIRTHDAYS

Ann Patchett

———— •◀ ▶•————

$\mathcal{H}$appy Christmases are all alike; every unhappy Christmas is unhappy in its own way. Or so it was in my family. There is a picture of a pretty, chubby toddler who was me, aged two, wearing a blue smocked dress in front of a blue flocked Christmas tree with dark blue glass balls (California circa 1965). My sister, Heather, age five and a half, is standing next to me in a red jumper. We look like girls who have plenty of presents and feel good about it. I don't remember this day, but it is documented. A few years later our parents were divorced. My mother moved us from Los Angeles to Tennessee, where she married my stepfather and we started a new life. Lying in bed late at night with my sister that first Christmas Eve in Nashville, a few weeks after I'd turned six, I told her I heard sleigh bells on the roof. She in turn dispelled me of what was nothing more than idle Santa gossip. In retrospect, I think that Christmas and Santa should be inextricably bound together by a thick rope so that when you throw one off the roof the other has no choice but to go crashing over the gutters as well. If I had to give up California and flocking and smocking and my father AND Santa Claus, it would have been infinitely easier to just give up Christmas.

But this is not a sad story about divorce or childhood. There were, after all, plenty of happy days. Flip through the photo album of memory and there we are: skating a little Sunfish across the lake in the silvery light of noon, or riding our horses, Sundance and Midnight, bareback through the woods. On balance, we were as happy or unhappy as any other family we knew. It was only our Christmases that were worse. For almost every other moment, we had mastered that level of normalcy that reconfigured families aspire to, but the season of peace and goodwill toward men unfailingly sent us straight to the pits. The lion's share of the blame for this must rest on the shoulders of my stepfather, a good man who probably could not help but ruin the holidays for the rest of us because he himself had endured Christmases so biblically dreadful that he knew no other way. The lynchpin of this entire story lies in the fact that my stepfather shared a birthday with the baby Jesus, and so spent his entire childhood without a birthday present or a birthday party or even a nice birthday wish from his mother. Every Christmas wreath and stocking and package wrapped in reindeer-covered paper dredged up the whole horrible memory for him again, so that by

Christmas morning he was nothing but a blur of grief. There was always a good bit of weeping beneath the tree in Tennessee.

There was weeping in California as well, as Christmas was the day that brought my otherwise stoically divorced father to his stoic knees. As soon as we heard the phone ring on Christmas morning, my sister and I would begin to sob like Pavlov's depressed dogs. We didn't like being so far away from him, but most of the year we lived with it. On Christmas morning we couldn't live with it another minute. My father would cry and we would cry in turns, first my sister, as she was older, then me; then we would hand the receiver back and forth a few times to cry harder and louder just because we couldn't help ourselves. We'd stay on until the whole phone was so thoroughly soaked that once I asked my sister if we might be electrocuted. She said I was an idiot.

My mother did her fair share of crying, too, in part out of sheer sympathy for the rest of us and in part because my stepfather's four children from his first marriage arrived every year on Christmas Day. Coincidentally, they lived in California not far from my father, although they didn't know him, a fact that all of the children found puzzling. Every year my stepsiblings (a boy and a girl slightly older than me, a girl and a boy slightly younger) spent Christmas on a plane so as to split the day between their parents. When they got to the house they always seemed happy at

first, diving into their presents with real energy and interest, but then, one by one, they'd start to realize it was
Christmas and their mother was on the other side of the
country alone. That was the point at which they put their
new baseball mitts and board games aside and began their
own weeping. I would move into my sister's room, where I
would sleep with my stepsisters, Tina and Angie, while my
stepbrothers, Mikey and Billy, moved into my room. My
sister, Heather, would move into the walk-in linen closet,
where she'd sleep on a pile of towels until everyone went
home again.

As bad as this situation was, there was one year very
early on when we tried it another way, and the other way
was worse. My stepfather surprised us all by taking us to
California. My mother and sister and I thought we were
taking him to the airport to fly out to visit his children, but
when we unloaded the luggage from the trunk I noticed
that the corner of my favorite quilted bathrobe, the white
one with the little rosebuds embroidered on it, was hanging
out of one of his suitcases. Why, I wanted to know, a tremor
of hysteria creeping into my voice, why was my stepfather
taking my bathrobe to California? To give it to one of his
daughters for Christmas? It was then he confessed that we
were all going together, as a family.

Except, of course, there had to be a drop-off. The children had to change hands, and that was tricky because the
stepfather didn't want to see the father, who most certainly

didn't want to see the stepfather with the mother. It was finally decided that my sister and I would be left with my stepfather's parents, the originators of Bad Christmas, while my mother and stepfather went safely away. We spent a stupendously miserable afternoon with these people, who were packing for their own Christmas Carribean holiday. They were noticeably less than pleased to have temporarily inherited the two little girls from the second marriage of their son for whom they never bought a birthday present. After our father got off of work, he came to the bottom of their steep driveway and we were sent down the hill to him, lugging our suitcases. That night we discovered that along with our bathrobes, our stepfather had packed the entire contents of our sock and underwear drawers. Nothing else.

After that, we stayed in Tennessee and did things the old-fashioned way. We had moved to a shockingly modern house built in the side of a hill far away in the country. The house was so poorly assembled that often large patches of mushrooms sprang up unexpectedly in the shag carpet of my sister's bedroom in the summer, forcing her to move back into the linen closet. In the winter, all the little mice in the fields walked in beneath the uneven wallboard and settled into sofa cushions for their long winter's nap. Our first Christmas in the country, my mother and stepfather thought we should turn our backs on commercialism and make all of our Christmas presents. While my mother sewed comforters and my sister and I knit slippers and pot holders, my stepfather was more ambitious. He got himself some wax and, using a set of surgical tools (he was a surgeon, so they were easy to come by), he made a group of tiny initials for the girls' earrings: an *H* and a *P* for my sister, Heather, a *T* and a *G* for Tina, an *A* and a *G* for Angie. For the boys, he shaped wax rings, and for me, who never had my ears pierced, he made a single large *A* that could hang from a chain. After he had the wax cast into molds, he sifted out all the bits and pieces of gold he could find in the Box of Important Things he kept on his dresser—some old fillings that had been pulled from his teeth, the wedding ring from his first marriage, class rings from high school and college—and had them all melted together. Afterward, we wore these amalgamations of my stepfather's personal history from necks and fingers and ears.

In the spirit of keeping things homemade, and because my mother hadn't had room in the car for Christmas ornaments when we drove away from California, the tree was decorated in strands of popcorn and cranberries that took us a week to string. We baked hooks into sugar cookies cut into the shape of stars and then frosted them yellow. We chose candy canes over foil tinsel, and when it was done we stepped back and breathed in our *Little House on the Prairie* triumph. As did the mice. By the next morning the lower branches were stripped of snacks, and the day after that the tree was clean up to knee level. I dreamed of star-shaped cookies scampering across the living room as if propelled along on their own tiny feet. They rounded the corner into the laundry room and disappeared under the dryer. Mouse H.Q. The mice shimmied up the trunk and took away the popcorn and the cranberries piece by piece, and though they could not lift the candy canes from their branches, they could stand on their back legs and nibble the lower ones until their collective mouse breath was pepperminty fresh. In the end, we stripped off what they'd left behind, the candy canes and bare strings and gnawed wire hooks, and had a naked tree that Christmas. We all thought it looked very natural.

The next year we employed our learning curve: scratch the homemade gifts (we were out of gold anyway), build a better mousetrap. This year there were boxes of rat poison nestled among the shiny presents, enabling us to keep our little prairie Christmas tree. We hung our cookies with impunity, and everything was pretty again. What nobody counted on was that the mice, who had come in for the winter to get warm, didn't much feel like going back outside to die in the snow. Instead, they crawled into the walls of the loamy house and breathed in their last breath of Christmas. The stench of death was so overpowering that we had to wrap up in blankets and leave the doors open for air. It was then that the aunts and uncles and cousins of the dead mice came in and ate the cookies.

Though the verses were different, the chorus of the song never changed: our father was far away, our stepfather had always lost out to the Christ child for birthday recognition, the unhappy stepsiblings appeared like clockwork and forced my sister into the closet. My mother, ever hopeful that what was bad could be made better, decided to strike Christmas from the month of December once and for all. The year before, she had tried moving my stepfather's birthday to June 25, throwing a summertime barbecue where friends sang the Happy Birthday song and brought presents, but he didn't fall for it. It wasn't his birthday, and therefore the good wishes were hollow. Christmas, then, should be the holiday to get the boot. For one year, December 25 would be a day for my stepfather alone. There would not be the slightest mention of Santa or Jesus. There would be no sweet potatoes, no baked ham studded with pineapple and cloves. It was going to be one whole round-the-clock birthday, with birthday hats and birthday wrapping paper only and homemade chocolate birthday cake. An entire lifetime of wrongs would finally be set right! Actually, I remember this as one of the better Christmases of my childhood because for once we simply didn't try. My mother said it was really much more logical to celebrate the Feast of the Magi, a holiday tailor made for gift exchange and conveniently located on January 6. Among the many unforeseen benefits to the celebration of the Epiphany was the fact that a Christmas tree (known that year as the "Magi tree") could be picked up for free at any grocery store or Boy Scout tree-selling kiosk after the twenty-fifth and that all presents could be purchased with after-Christmas discounts. When my father called tearfully to wish us a Merry Christmas that year, we explained to him that the deal was off. We were celebrating the stepfather's birthday.

"What about the Christmas presents I sent?" my father asked.

"We're saving them for the Feast of the Magi," my sister said.

My father explained to us that what he had sent were Christmas presents, not Magi presents, and that we were to go upstairs to our rooms and open them immediately.

But was that the right thing to do, seeing as how this year was only and completely the stepfather's birthday?

"Now," my father said.

The Magi angle didn't seem to stick, and by the next year we were back to business as usual. Even though I was only eleven at the time, I had long since reached the point where Christmas made me insanely nervous. One night a few days before Christmas I woke up in such a sweaty state of panic I could not go back to sleep. By the soft glow of the plug-in night-light in its baseboard socket, I decided it might make me feel better if I could unwrap a single present that my father had sent to me and then wrap it back up again. The gifts were in my bedroom, so it wasn't much of a problem. If a package is disassembled slowly and reassembled precisely, who ever knows the difference? I took my time. I carefully slid off the ribbon and peeled back the tape. I was surprised to find that this small act of defiance made me feel calmer immediately. Now there was something I didn't have to wonder about, to worry about: my father had gotten me a sweater and a matching skirt. I didn't like them, but I found it comforting to know in advance that I didn't like them. The next night I opened the other two presents he'd sent: a stuffed Siamese cat and the game of Life, both of which were much better choices. I didn't care what I was getting for Christmas, but somehow knowing in advance made me feel I had a secret life, one in which I could watch the pageant of Christmas with critical detachment. I slipped back into bed and felt happy.

But the peace never seemed to last. The next night I was up again. I felt the encroaching holiday circle my throat like a cord of tiny blinking lights pulled tight. I had to go downstairs. I had to get under the tree.

This was no small task. While mice could roam the house freely (we never used poison again), the human beings were more or less electronically confined to their rooms. We had a complex security system that included weight-sensitive pads secreted in different locations underneath the wall-to-wall carpeting. The only Off switch was hidden behind my stepfather's night table. To get downstairs, I had to cling to the banister that overlooked the sunken living room. As long as I could feel the bite of the carpet tacks on the balls of my feet, I knew I was off the alarm pad. Inching along step by step, I took about thirty minutes to make it down the hall and then down the stairs. By then my nerves were in such bad shape that I had to unwrap and rewrap several presents, presents that weren't even mine, before I felt calm enough to try to make it back to my room again. The second night, when I was halfway down the hall, I remembered a thoroughly rotten little boy, the son of my stepfather's friends, who had taught all six of the children how to squeeze between two banister rails and jump down onto the sofa twenty feet below. His family had been to see us the summer before, when my stepsiblings were visiting, and at one unfortunate point, all of the children were left alone together in the house. One by one he shoved us through the railings, except for my oldest stepbrother, Mikey, who was too big and so had to go over the top.

On that night before Christmas there was plenty of moonlight with which to locate the couch, and saying a prayer for the souls of any mice who might have been sleeping in the cushions, I flung myself into the darkness to speed up the process of maniacal unwrapping. If I had missed by a foot or so and hit the coffee table instead, leaving my family to find my broken body on the living room floor in the morning, they would have just assumed I'd had enough of Christmas. Instead, I survived the jump year after year, and everyone always wondered why I was so hard to surprise. I'd hold up a box on Christmas morning, close my eyes, and give the thing a shake. "Hat and gloves," I'd say, and everyone would marvel at the way I always seemed to know exactly what was coming up next, even though technically such knowledge should have been impossible.

THE ACCIDENTAL SANTA

Joni Rodgers

———— ◆ ————

I had stopped believing in Santa Claus long before his powder-blue Buick Skylark ripped through a busy intersection in Allentown, Pennsylvania, clipped the back of a pickup truck, bolted over the curb, and slammed into the corner of an abandoned gas station.

The gray day was filled with stinging, sleetish precipitation. Too cold for rain, too ill-natured for snow. I'd pulled into the empty parking lot to salvage a few of the carefully decorated Christmas cookies my daughter had just dumped out of a foil gift box and onto the backseat of the car as we rushed, late as usual, to her preschool Christmas pageant.

"Oh, Jerusha! God bless America." I was better at biting back my cuss words back then.

"I want a cookie," she sobbed.

"We fixed them up all pretty for the bake sale. Now look. Who'll want these?"

"I will!" My girl. Always willing to sacrifice for the greater good. And so quick on the uptake, it made me laugh out loud.

That's when the Skylark and pickup truck connected with a *pop* on the street in front of us. That frozen puff of laughter was still hanging in the air. The old Buick hit the wall eighteen or twenty feet away. I felt the shock wave, the noise of it. Then that altered-time sense in which images (*crumpled metal, buckling bricks*) become gut response before they translate to actual perception and, finally, a semi-reasoned impulse to help.

Leaving Jerusha latched in her car seat, I scrambled across a crusty, brown snowbank toward the Skylark. A strange odor steamed from the angled hood. Not gasoline. Something slick and transmissiony. The old man behind the wheel was weeping and frantically pushing on the deeply indented door. His false teeth were half out. Blood flowed from his mouth and nose into his long, white whiskers, spattering dark spots on red velvet, red spots on white trim; making a horror movie costume out of the most recognizable ensemble between here and the North Pole.

Santa Claus.

I called for help. Cars on the slushy street slowed but kept going. Someone rolled down her window and shouted that she was calling 911. The truck driver sat in the cab of his pickup, beating back the air bag, yelling something about *F-ing old coot don't know the brakes from the gas.* Santa battered his hand against the spider-veined window. I braced my foot on the side of the car and yanked until the door groaned open.

"Someone's coming," I said. "Stay calm."

He seized my hand, croaking and babbling in some Slavic language. Or maybe the language of panic; an utterly foreign expression of how baffling it is to suddenly find your face in tatters. He leaned against me, and I stroked his long, white hair.

"Here," I said, "let me tuck this jacket around you."

But as I shucked my winter coat off my shoulders, he swung his legs out of the car, grasped my torso, and pulled himself up. He wasn't a fat man, but he was a head taller than me and much fuller than he'd looked folded into the driver's seat.

"No! Sir, please! Do you speak English? Please, keep still. The ambulance is—"

He swayed, then slumped heavily against me. I did my best to steer our trajectory as we awkwardly stumbled back onto a jagged bank of snow and mud left by the street plow. We ended up in a clumsy Pietà; me with one coat sleeve still on, him laid out across my lap, still grasping the waist of my sage-green dress.

"Crap!" I whispered. "Please, Jesus . . . shit . . . tell me what to do."

Santa didn't move. I yanked my coat the rest of the way off and spread it over him. Wadding part of my full pleated skirt in my hand, I gingerly applied pressure to his stream-ing nose. I know nothing about first aid, but that seemed like a first aid–ish idea. Apply pressure. Santa made a small, wet sound, breathing through his shattered mouth.

"Schum schie, schum schie . . ."

I am a mother, not an EMT. When in doubt, we lullaby. This little German carol I'd learned in grade school always soothed my children when I rocked them in their footie PJs.

"Joseph dearest, Joseph mine, help me cradle this child di-vine."

"Mommy?" Jerusha called from the open car door. "What's the matter with Santa?"

"He, um . . . he bumped his nose," I called back to her. "He's resting for a sec. You stay in the car."

"Can I see?" She craned forward, trying to get a better look.

"*No!* Stay in the car, Jerusha."

"I want to give Santa a cookie."

"Not right now, Twinkie. Santa doesn't feel good."

"Can I have a cookie?"

"Sure. But stay in the car. I'm watching you."

"Is *Santa* watching me?"

"Yes! Santa is watching! And he told me . . . he says . . ." Oh, I hate those little lies. I had vowed I would *not* be a mother who manipulated her children with those little hop-toad lies that leap so easily to the tongue. "He says if you get out of that car . . . he'll be *seriously pissed!*"

She nodded solemnly and pulled the door shut.

The sprung trunk of Santa's Skylark bobbed in the wind, which riffled up bright red bows and Mickey Mouse wrapping paper. On the dashboard lay a street map of the city and a beat-up leather Day-Timer. Santa probably knew he was too old to be driving around in a world where no one yields the right of way to reindeer. Probably found himself having to check his list more than twice lately. He was an old man. But he was an old man on a mission.

"Schum schie, schum schie . . ."

I was wearing patterned tights that matched my dress, but my skirt had billowed up when we fell. My legs felt raw and freezer-burned against the icy embankment. We waited the same eternity it takes for the teakettle to whistle. Finally, the sound of sirens came, and then came closer. Father Christmas gripped my hand.

"They're coming," I said.

The ambulance skidded to a stop, and the attendant strode toward me, lugging a white plastic case in one hand, using the other to gesticulate as he spoke with a Jersey accent.

"How stupid are you, lady?" He launched into a litany of my unforgivable gaffes, from "takin' the victim outta the goddamn car" to "lettin' a total stranger bleed all over ya" and other things that "any pinhead knows from junior high health class." I didn't bother explaining that in parochial school, health education was preempted for abstinence-only indoctrination, primarily concerned with "the devil, the world, and our sinful flesh."

"Will he be okay?" I asked.

"No thanks to you," the ambulance attendant assured me.

Meanwhile, two other EMTs rushed over, dragging an assortment of equipment. Once the first guy had completed a perfunctory exam on Father Christmas, they carefully maneuvered him onto a gurney and took him away. I got up, shaking, partly because of the cold, partly because the human body does that when it realizes the person it embodies has been changed.

"I'm gonna need a statement from you," a policeman called from the curb, but I pretended not to hear him. I crunched back through the dirty snow to my car and opened the door. Jerusha looked up at me with big brown eyes, her mouth and both hands full of gingerbread.

"You shed I could haff a cookie."

I gave my statement to the officer, who stuffed my bloody coat into a trash bag as if it were evidence in a case of foul play. We'd already missed the preschool luncheon, but I figured we might still make the program, even if I stopped to buy a clean dress.

"C'mon, c'mon," I mumbled, cruising up the frontage road. "There's a friggin' Wal-Mart jammed into every crevice of the known universe. There's gotta be a Wal-Mart around here."

"There!" Jerusha pointed.

Uncanny. The child was a shopper from day one.

"Mommy! You're pulling!" she complained as I dragged her across the parking lot.

"C'mon!" I barked. "We're in a hurry!"

"My shoes are gonna get wet," she whined. "Carry me!"

"No. I don't want to stain your dress."

"If I get a stain on my dress, can I get a new one?" she asked.

"No." And knowing how her mind worked, I added, "Don't even think about it."

"*You* get a new dress," she wailed, dragging her feet. "Why don't I get a new dress?"

"You get a new dress every five minutes! You're *wearing* a brand-new dress! Now *C'MON!*"

First the lies. Then the barking. Now I was yanking her along by her little candy cane arm. Obviously, years of therapy stretched out in front of this child like industrial gray carpet between aisles of plastic wise men and flocked fake trees in Wal-Mart's Holiday Center. I joylessly selected a cheap blue shirtdress and asked the clerk if I could leave my soiled dress and tights in the trash can behind the fitting-room counter.

"No," she said, crinkling her eyebrows together. "But here."

She primly held out a plastic bag. I took it, changed, and shoved my bloodied clothes into her trash can when she wasn't looking.

"Merry fucking Christmas," I mumbled.

"You said the *F* word," Jerusha saw fit to mention. "If you get to say the *F* word—"

"Don't even think it."

We arrived at the preschool just in time for her to run up and join her class onstage singing "Jazzy Jingle Bells." There was a little play about a snowperson family, and a few other songs that carefully avoided saying anything that might mean anything. All adorable, of course, but it felt so empty. As the children sang "We Wish You a Happy Holiday," inoculating the traditional lyrics with stilted rhythm, Santa burst into the back of the room, hefting a huge bag of Little Golden Books, which the Mothers of Preschoolers had wrapped and garnished with curly ribbon at our last MOP meeting.

"Ho Ho Ho! Merry Christmas!" he bellowed, and parents crowded around, waiting to photo/video-document their child's meeting with Santa. But I'd left my camera in the car, I realized, so I just stood there lamely when he lifted Jerusha to his lap. She stared intently at his face, reached up, touched his nose. I could tell by the look on her face that she had awakened from the dreamiest part of her childhood.

———————

My own awakening had come in second grade. On the last day of school before Christmas vacation, I sat cross-legged with the rest of my classmates in the Story Corner of Mrs.

Glenmar's classroom at Mount Calvary Evangelical Elementary. Cold winter sunlight spilled across the linoleum floor. With her crown of blue hair, stumpy orthopedic shoes, and a spray of jingle bells on her green dress, Mrs. Glenmar looked as festive and welcoming as a fake Wal-Mart Christmas tree. We wriggled and giggled with excitement as she pressed floppy felt letters onto a nubby board. They stuck as if they were made of magic, and because we were big enough to know important stuff like letters, we called each one out loud.

"S-A-N-T-A!"

"Who can tell me who that is?" said Mrs. Glenmar with that winkishly conspiratorial expression adults wear all December long.

"*Santa!*" we cried in hyper-ecstatic holiday shrill.

"That's right!" said Mrs. Glenmar. "And who can tell me who *this* is?"

She slowly rearranged the letters, but this time, the spelling-along was a lot less enthusiastic.

"S-A-T-a-n."

"Anyone?" Something about the arch of her eyebrow said, *Answer, or face the lake of fire.*

"Satan?" I volunteered meekly, because all my classmates were sitting there with their little peppermint pink mouths hanging open.

"That's right. *SAY-TAN,*" Mrs. Glenmar enunciated. She went on to explain how Father Christmas was a lie invented by the Pope, who served the Father of All Lies, and anyone who believed in Santa was stealing baby Jesus's birthday. And that made Jesus very sad. She looked up at the plaster-cast crucifix on the wall near her framed and autographed eight-by-ten glossy of President Nixon (who'd recently been reelected by the will of God). Our eyes followed, but quickly slid away from the Savior's wounded expression. To get crucified by Jews and have your birthday stolen by Catholics—well, no wonder he always looked so mournful.

I didn't cry. I wasn't a crybaby like all those other kids. And I loved Jesus! No way was I a sniveling little birthday-stealer. A few kids tried to present repudiating evidence. Thumpy noises. Mysteriously vanishing Oreos and milk. Someone's daddy had actually stepped in reindeer drop-pings! But my eyes were open now—even before Mrs. Glenmar explained that sometimes adults lie to children for reasons we would understand when we grew up. And when I grew up, I did understand.

Twenty-some Christmases later, I also learned the true story of Santa.

I was playing the Virgin Mary (oh, shut up) in a tradi-tional Elizabethan miracle play at a little theater in Bethle-hem, Pennsylvania. (Pennsylvania's Bethlehem is to Messianic birthplaces what fake Christmas trees are to a pine forest, but it's close enough for about eight hundred million tourists, so local artists make the most of it.) My friend Rita Lipsitz was playing the angel Gabriel. I loved

Rita, even though it took a lot of energy to quash my kids' giggling at her name. She was a brilliant artist who (when she wasn't struggling with the anti-gestalt of being a Jew announcing the birth of Christ) taught liberal-artsy college courses like Renaissance Poetry, Ecclesiastics, and Dance History. I got smarter just having coffee with her.

My husband worked nights, including that particular Christmas Eve, and Rita was a single mom, so she and I decided to get together for an amalgamated festivity we called Hanuchristmakah, which included: little gifts from the Everything's 99 Cents! store; stockings stuffed with kosher candy; and an interesting mix of holiday carols and Broadway show tunes. Rita and I sipped wine in my kitchen, watching the kids decorate cookies with tinted frosting, red licorice strings, and sprinkles. Just before midnight, we lit our menorah, tucked baby Jesus in the manger, and set out treats for Santa. (Actually, it was more like a quarter to nine, but we told the kids it was midnight, and they believed it, not because they were gullible but because they were guileless.)

"Do your kids still believe in Santa?" I asked Rita, once the children were nestled all snug in their beds, while visions surgically inserted by multimillion-dollar advertising campaigns danced in their heads.

"What's not to believe?" she said. "He was a real guy. A Turkish bishop. Nicholas of Izmir. Legend has it, some nobleman couldn't afford dowries for his three daughters, so one night, the bishop threw a bag of gold through the window to cover the first daughter's marriage. Second night, he pitched in enough for the second girl. Third night, finding the window closed, he dropped the third daughter's gift down the chimney to the fireplace, where stockings were hanging to dry, and the rest is history."

"No way," I said. "If a member of the unfunded gentry received gold via an open window two nights in a row, there's no way he's closing that window the third night."

"Coldhearted skeptics notwithstanding," said Rita pointedly, "the legend is in keeping with the bishop's documented reputation for benevolence. I mean, they don't just canonize any old fart off the street. Nicholas is the patron saint of those who love Christmas most: children, bakers, and pawnbrokers."

"We didn't have saints," I said. "We had lawn ornaments. Blow-mold nativity scenes."

"Blow mold?"

"Yeah. Those hollow plastic figures with lightbulbs inside. I've been searching eBay for a blow-mold holy family. Three blow-mold wise men. Blow-mold shepherds kneeling before a blow-mold baby Jesus in his little blow-mold manger."

"You'd never put something that kitschy in your yard," said Rita. "You just like saying *blow-mold baby Jesus*."

"Well, yeah."

"My kids want one of those ten-foot inflatable Santas with the fan unit in the base that keeps him nice and rotund. You have to tether him to a tree so he doesn't topple over onto the plywood reindeer. And you hate for the kids to see Santa tied to a tree, but what can you do? A legend that overblown has to be anchored to something solid."

"True that." I raised my glass to the Gospel According to Rita Lipsitz.

———— • ————

We like our cultural icons big. A Santa larger than life. A Jesus larger than death. We present them as Sebastian Cabot and Fabio, though they actually looked more like Trini Lopez and Osama bin Laden. We make them white so we're not troubled by our innate racism. We make them supernatural so we're not pressured to live up to their example. But in reality, both these guys were about love, not magic. At the base of the grandiloquent image of Jolly Old Saint Nicholas resides a quietly persistent habit of human kindness. And nestled long ago in the real-life manger was an extraordinarily ordinary newborn boy, who inspired more than a legend when he inspired Nicholas of Izmir.

He inspired a man to become a saint. To love his neighbor. To give and give and, without recognition or thanks, give again. To hitch a sleigh to his good intentions and to brave snowy rooftops. To venture out onto icy streets behind the wheel of a powder-blue Buick he was far too frail to drive.

"Joseph dearest, Joseph mine, help me cradle this child divine . . ."

The battered Santa and I breathed soft clouds, waiting for the sirens.

"Schum schie . . . schum schie . . ."

How odd, in that moment, to find myself so comforted by this little song from a church I thought had scarred me. But in life's most metal-twisting moments, we often retreat to our traditions. Dormant faith awakens to meet crushing need, and the contrast is as sharply drawn as the disparate sensations of hard ice beneath me and the warm weight of St. Nicholas in my arms.

Christmas surrounded us like a snow globe, and it was undeniably real. Cold. Lullabies. Blood. The authenticity of care, when one is caring for a stranger.

I closed my eyes and purposely returned to the dream of believing.

CHRISTMAS 2001

Anne Giardini

———◆——

*I*t has only just occurred to me that there might be
some profit in re-creating the worst Christmas of
my life beyond the potential inspiration of a blossom of
schadenfreude within the breastbones of my readers. Most
of life—even the parts that should be encased in concrete
and dropped to the bottom of an abandoned salt mine in
New Mexico until they have ceased to pulse with a toxic,
incandescent gleam—most of life has at least the possibility
of inducing an increase in wisdom, if held up to scrutiny,
and wisdom is the only worthwhile consolation I am aware
of for getting older. Even the worst events of our personal
slice of history might, if brought out from time to time and
subjected to examination, have something more to tell us
than just how much misery we are capable of withstanding
without being permanently broken. There is also always
the possibility that there is something linguistically significant in the suitcase of the word *recover;* that to recover a

memory fully brings with it the possibility of fully recovering from it.

Several holiday seasons present themselves to my line and hook as I cast back over the years. There was the Christmas when I was a child, one of five, all of us under age twelve and all felled with a strain of flu that induced muscle pains, lethargy, and violent vomiting. My parents took turns pressing damp cloths onto our brows and murmuring comforting words while we discharged the acid contents of our stomachs into bowls. When Christmas morning came, I moaned to my mother—feebly, pathetically—that I was too sick to open my presents. But the truth of the matter is that I was in thrall at that time to Louisa May Alcott's *Little Women* and was not too weak or delirious to fail to appreciate how pleasingly Beth-like was my pallor and languor, and not too far gone to enjoy the private documentary short that unscrolled inside my aching eyes: my brother and my sisters, sobbing at my funeral, contrite at last for all their sins against me.

Another contender is the Christmas about ten years later, when I was nineteen and took a Greyhound to a large U.S. city to see a loutish boyfriend who had fallen asleep and failed to meet me at the bus depot. The bus got in at ten at night, and the pimps and drug dealers on whose turf I had been discharged began to encircle tender, wide-eyed me with growing menace until, just before midnight, I had enough sense to get another bus out of town. But wait, that wasn't Christmas exactly. I recall now the driver of that second bus turning in his seat and announcing "Happy New Year" to his three passengers—we sat as far from one another as possible, each in his or her own dark, rumbling misery—as the clock ticked over into the year 1979. I remember the chafe of the driver's cheerful voice, although I see now that he might simply have been making the best of it. The night got worse in fact, because, when I arrived at the door of my boyfriend's mother's house—she had offered to take me in for the night—I spilled out on her threshold my story about the big black pimps who had been threatening me only an hour before. Hundreds of them, eight feet tall at least, dressed in shiny leisure suits, with fat gold rings and chains. It was only when I stepped into her kitchen that I saw her New Year's Eve guests still at the dinner table, most of them black, their conversation entirely interrupted by my noisy, plangent arrival.

The Christmas at the end of the year 1986 had the potential to be the worst. My parents were spending a sabbatical year in Paris in a rented apartment, and all five of their children, in our twenties by then, traveled to France to camp on their floors and couches. There had been sporadic bomb attacks in Paris over the past year, and I remember that my brother was nervous about attending Christmas Eve services at the American Church in Paris, but we went anyway, and we all sang noisily and off-key. "Joy to the World," "O Come O Come, Emmanuel." It was, I believe, the year of the greatest labor unrest in France since the worker and student uprisings of 1968. Rolling strikes interrupted the electricity, the buses, the trains, the subways. But, for us, all of this had a glamorous Parisian cast to it. We practiced the art of the Gallic shrug until we thought we had it mastered, the *Qu'est-ce qu'on peut faire?* upward shift of the eyebrows, the pursed lips, the dislocation of the molecules of inconvenience from this earthly plane out into the stratosphere by means of a readjustment of the vertebrae and neck, every minor nuisance and difficulty sent spinning with a lift of the chin. Over the days between Christmas and New Year, peace broke out. Algerian terrorists took a break from bomb-making. Perhaps, like us, they were drinking cold glasses of Beaujolais nouveau and small cups of scalding coffee in the local cafés, and thinking of gold and frankincense instead of fertilizer and fuel oil. I stayed with my boyfriend in a friend's apartment with a sideways view of the Eiffel Tower from her tiny wrought-iron balcony. We got engaged and then made our way to Italy, where he was living then, on a train whose engineers were not on strike but whose ticket-takers were, so we got all the way back to Florence without having to pay so much as a sou. Not the worst Christmas by far.

Another jump forward, to the end of 2001. A miserable year, memorable for its earthquakes, terrorist attacks, wildfires, drought, war, and human rights outrages. A year that will be remembered for our collective retreat from the idea of the global village, a time characterized by a constriction of the human heart, by suspicion, by doubt, by fear of the shadowy other. At the end of this year, my family gathered on Galiano Island to mark what we understood would be my mother's last Christmas. She was dying of breast cancer, and we had been told that she would not last long into the next year.

Galiano is one of British Columbia's Gulf Islands, a stretch of islands scattered like dice in the Strait of Georgia, between Vancouver Island and the mainland. The islands are made of coarse rocks that were formed by volcanoes millions of years ago in the Pacific Ocean. They then hitched a slow ride eastward on the earth's shifting plates toward the coast. Galiano is six miles long, and narrow, only a mile and a half at its widest. Its Web site (www.galianoisland.com) proclaims it as "glorious in spring, especially for naturalists and bird watchers. Wild flowers flourish in the forests and above the shores, and migrating birds visit on their way to summer nesting grounds." The fall is also highlighted as "a time of golden light, ripe berries and the northern birds returning south. The days are still warm, the air is fragrant and rain is rare before November."

What the Web site implies in its omission is the fact that Galiano is grim almost beyond bearing in the winter. Darkness falls in the evenings at five o'clock, and the sun will not reappear until eight the next morning. Most days, the sun is notional at best, shrouded in layer upon layer of thick, gray cloud. Only one in four days goes without its squall or storm. Dampness is pervasive. Everything is sodden or dripping or clammy. The ground underfoot is saturated. Rain falls from the spreading branches of the trees—Douglas fir, western red cedar, alder, lodgepole pine—and collects in the understory of salal, sword fern, and Oregon grape. The constant damp encourages wild excesses of growth. Bunchgrass, elderberry, saskatoon, rabbitbrush, skunk cabbage, loosestrife, foamflower, and twinflower all compete for soil and sun and space. The twisted branches of arbutus reach to the water's edge, and reeds, sedges, and glasswort thrive at the margin, where the green ocean waters slop against the sand and rocks. The landscape is uncontained, an unceasing roil of growth and rot, regrowth and decay.

We arrived in several groups a day or two before Christmas—husbands, wives, children, gifts, clothes, and supplies—and found that the several cottages we had booked were the opposite of what the word *cottage* brings to mind. They were ramshackle, cold, and dirty. The beds were lumpy, the sheets dubious or worse. Years of cooking grease coated the stovetops. The pots were black, the floors sticky, the couches repellent, the windows gray and unwashed. There was no charm or comfort or beauty.

And yet we stayed. In fact, as I recall it, no one seriously pursued trying to find an alternative. We were twelve adults and almost as many children. We were constrained by the ferry schedule, and in any case, there was unlikely to be anyplace else that could have taken us all at such short notice. A part of the reason we didn't make any effort to leave may have been because the cottages, in fact the entire island, so perfectly reflected the way we felt—dismal, broken, incapable of giving or receiving consolation. We also sensed that we had put our mother through enough to come here; we could not ask her to be dislodged again for our own convenience when she had not known ease or freedom from grief for many months. None of this was spoken, but I know we all felt it, down to the youngest children.

We didn't even try to set the place in order. Instead, the adults, except for my mother, drank steadily, beginning before noon. We must have produced meals, bathed and fed the children, had discussions, played board games and put together puzzles, prepared stockings, opened gifts on Christmas morning—but I have retained none of this. What I remember is pouring a glass of Scotch every day and ensuring that the bitter liquid was never quite gone until it was replaced with wine before dinner.

I remember seeing my mother sitting on one of those horrible couches and realizing how far advanced was the withdrawal of the heat that all my life she had radiated like a brazier. She had been the center of our gravity, had prevented things from falling apart, had kept conversation spilling, had always brought her wit gently to bear. And now she sat carefully, holding herself still, wearing what we thought of as her cancer face; radiation and steroids and pain had replaced her rapid, true expressions with a guarded absence. She was in retreat from us, and there was almost no will left in her.

I thought then back to when my husband and I lived in the British Columbia interior, when, in mid-October, we took the children to the Adams River salmon run. We watched as thousands of determined salmon, utterly uncaring of us, battled their way upstream toward oblivion. The river was red with them. The waters boiled with their struggles. Salmon that had lost the strength to get to their destination, doomed salmon, littered the riverbanks, and these salmon rapidly lost their rosy color; they were gray and gaping, and their eyes stared up to the merciless sky. These were the ones that my mother made me think of. Not the fighting ones but the ones that had not quite made it.

I do not remember what we talked about during those three days, but I do recollect how words felt in my mouth:

cold, marmoreal, weighted like stone. I think most of these heavy words were left unsaid. I would go to sit beside my silent mother and fall into silence too, not companionably, but in despair.

I can remember only one moment of delight from that time. On the afternoon of the day before we left, a cold winter sun briefly appeared. We all left my mother and walked, carrying and shepherding children, along the only road, following it toward the north end of the island. As we passed a frozen pond, a rough, black circle ringed with the dried stalks and husks of summer plants, one of the children, or it might have been me, threw a large pebble to test the ice. The stone landed, then bounced and bounced again, and as it did, a ringing noise resounded, like frozen laughter released from a hidden underwater chamber. A hopeful, joyous, ridiculous sound. We stood there in a group, throwing fist-sized rocks onto the frozen surface of the pond, making it ring and chime, and gulping in the cold ice-music together with the frigid air. I stayed behind for a long time after the others had walked on, wholly contained within the rhythm of throwing and listening, like a fisherman casting his line again and again in hope of a catch. For almost an hour, alone, I held off the relentless advance of time.

THE BITE BEFORE CHRISTMAS

Stanley Bing

———————

'*ve* never been a huge fan of the holidays. I like Christmas as a cultural event, full of figgy pudding and jolly, scabrous Santas hawking redemption on every street corner and then a week of limbo-weirdness in which nobody works, ending with a drunken, hurling crowd assembling in the public square for the change of year that, in the end, means nothing. The music of the season is nice, too, except when it makes you feel like crying. And I don't mind the savings you get at the major department stores, either.

But starting at Thanksgiving time, I always begin to feel like my life isn't as good as all the stuff I'm seeing in the popular media. Maybe my mom made a turkey that came out a little less succulent and more chewy than Martha's. Or the circle around the family table was a little too small, and growing smaller. Or the presents exchanged all around didn't fill anybody's hearts with the kind of joy commensurate with seasonal expectations, and in fact occasionally generated whatever the opposite of goodwill among men was supposed to be. "Oh, that's nice," the recipient would say, looking at the proffered object with brooding, abject melancholy. And in that moment, what was revealed was not the glowing finger of the miraculous or the omnipresence of a guiding love, but only the amazing power of everyday life to be, above all, its immutable self.

Noel is the time of giving and forgiveness and community and shared warmth by the fireside and true appreciation of all that speaks of the fullness that underlies the mundane. And to the extent that it actually does refract light against that evanescent ideal, it has always been a time of emotional peril, of stocktaking, of unwanted insight into what is not, as well as what is.

Being a wandering stranger in a merry Christian land hasn't added to the allure, either. My people came to this brave new American world about a hundred years ago, and found the orgy of red and green everywhere and their children totally left out of the whole baby Jesus thing. We were forced, being ever-competitive with whatever reigning culture into which we were being assimilated, to drum up our own version of the deal. Thus a minor holiday on our calendar, one that featured a few coins and nuts and fun games played with a spinning top, was promoted into a major feast of acquisition and gift-giving. This Not-Christmas has its own power to be both more and less than what we want it to be.

In the end, what I am left with when December rolls around and over us is a profound sense of not truly belonging to the game everybody else is playing, of missing . . . missing something, somebody . . . and a sense that somewhere, not very far away, someone is having a much better time.

So I don't always start from a very good place, is the point I'm making.

Which is not to say that I don't have great holidays to remember. I'm not Scrooge. The shopping part is nice, particularly when you imagine the rosy flush of tiny faces as they tear away the wrapping paper. And the nap after the festive meal is as deep as sleep can get without easing over into coma. And at last, there is, in addition to all the crusty stuff, the feeling, when one has a family, of that little group clinging to a raft against the tide of commercialism, fatuity, piety (both real and faux), and communal materialism that has become our annual Noel.

It may not be perfect, we think, but it's ours. And also, there is this thought, in the midst of it all—what if there was no Us? How terrible would that be? To see it on a midnight clear so starkly that there would be no way to deny it?

Would such a life be worth the living?

At the beginning of the new century, which did not spell the end of time, in spite of all predictions, I left my home of twenty-five years. I'm not the only guy of my age to do so, but there is no community of such people. We are alone, each and all, and never more alone than when the rest of the world is wrapping itself in one giant embrace.

It was some time in coming, this departure, and it represented, in its way, a simultaneous death and birth. The birth, unlike our genuine entry into this vale of laughter and tears, seems to be a somewhat protracted affair. The labor is still under way, at any rate, some years later. The death, on the other hand, like the actual moment that each of us will inevitably share, was short and brutal, even though the process leading to it was as long and as messy as that which attends the real thing. One minute I was in the world as I knew it. The next, I was not.

This took place in early December, when the Thanksgiving pumpkins had already begun to deflate on our porches, their grins rotting away from the bottom, turning to smirks and leers. It was cold. I had already secured for myself a small place in that most stereotypical location for men embarked on such a journey—an apartment on the marina. This was perhaps two miles from my old house, and as distant as the moon.

Christmas Eve arrived, as it inevitably does, whether retailers are ready for the end of shopping days or not. All the people with places to go went there and nestled into the bosoms of those closest to them, however capacious those bosoms might be. Those of us with no bosoms to go to were thrust out into the night.

There aren't many places open on Christmas Eve. Some restaurants are lit, their tables shoved together to accommodate entire clans tearing up some poor bird or other.

The occasional convenience store glimmers like a cheap toy, open for thoughtless, last-minute gift-givers, manned in my area by turbaned employees who presumably do not feel the misery of working on a day of comfort and joy. But the sidewalks are rolled up, all other stores dark. A few bereft individuals lurch here and there beneath the starry firmament. There is no traffic.

I was scheduled to go out of town the next morning, so that would be all right. But that evening, the void that underlies all of existence yawned wide and threatened to suck me in. Gooey treacle and pompous rejoicing oozed from the television. If I stayed indoors, the only solution would be to drink myself into a somnolent torpor, and I try to do that only when I'm happy.

I drove. No, I didn't want to go to my local bar, full of sad, empty losers whose lives echoed my own at that moment. No, I didn't want to play glow-in-the-dark miniature golf, which, for some reason, was open at that hour. And I didn't want to drive anywhere near my old house, full of warmth and light and, quite possibly, turkey that did not come packaged in its own microwavable gravy.

I went to the Thruway Diner. As it has been every day, 24-7, for the past fifty years, it was open. I went in, and was amazed. Quite a few people were there. The stools at the counter were relatively full. The tables, both in the fast-turnover front room and the more high-tone, less casual dining room out back, were not full to bursting, but there was life in them under the tinsel and felt caps festooned with fake fur that hung from the doorways. A little seasonal music driveled from the speakers, but a game of some kind was on the TV sets around the room.

I chose the counter, because I saw that it was fully loaded with lumpy dumpsters like myself, men in their prime, as I am, whose hair might not have been sufficiently combed for the evening, dressed in ski jackets, heavy shirts, and boots, each bent over a plate of something to their liking, food not determined by the propriety of the hour, the day, the time of year. The guy to my right was reading a three-day-old paper. He had waffles and sausages. A more studious individual to my left was reading a book in a language I couldn't guess at. It had no pictures. He was eating bacon and eggs.

I looked down the counter and saw the lineup of dishes selected by my brethren this Christmas Eve. There were perhaps ten of us. All but one was having breakfast at an hour when the rest of the world was staggering away from a table full of dinner, groaning with the strain that all that festivity was placing on their overloaded systems.

I don't know about you, pilgrim, but for me breakfast at dinnertime has always been the most comforting of meals. Some claim meatloaf with potatoes for that privilege. Others swear by turkey with all the fixin's. But for me there's nothing like a stack of buttermilk flapjacks with three kinds of carcinogenic meat to make me feel like there's a home someplace to which I just might be headed.

I had the flapjacks with bacon, ham, and sausage. Coffee, too. Not a word passed between any of us at that place where we shared our simple meal. In that silence was all the community that we required. Anything more would have been too much and far, far too little.

The next morning I took off for the coast. In a week, it would be the New Year, an enforced day of merriment I usually detest more than any other. On that Christmas morning, however, I found myself looking forward with a tiny flicker of cheer to the end of one twelve-month cycle and the beginning of the next. Some things are hard to leave behind, even when you have to. Maybe once that ritual is done, it doesn't hurt to rejoin the rest of the world to celebrate all the Noels that just might lie ahead.

SURVIVOR

Louis Bayard

───────◆────────

*A*t some point in our conversation, it occurred to me this was where they brought the shoplifters. Toxed-up junkies, nose-picking teenagers, thrill-seeking grannies . . . one after another, dragged with their contraband into this same windowless chamber with hard orange plastic-shell chairs and naked overhead lights. Forced to confess their crimes . . . cuffed . . . read their rights . . . probably by the very guy who was interrogating me now.

A lanky guy, bald as an elbow, with eyes like frozen mouse droppings. A straight mouth, a straight back. He was the kind of guy who'd been in the army with my dad. Give him a couple of martinis, he'd unbend—bring out the war stories—tell you about peeing next to General Westmoreland. Sober, he gave you nothing. *You* had to give.

He sat ten feet away from me in his orange shell chair, and he fixed his mouth in that straight line, and he said, with disarming softness, "What makes you think you should be Rudy the Reindeer?"

It was a question I was fully prepared to answer—I'd just written a mini-essay on the subject as part of my application—but in that moment, I foundered. If I were to be truly honest (and, from the looks of him, he could sniff out deceit), I would have to confess that I was here to save my life.

Which, apart from setting the wrong tone, would then require me to take him through all the links in my dark mental chain. The first being:

1. Actuarial Data

Somewhere toward the beginning of my sixteenth year, I read that more people committed suicide during the holidays than at any other time of year. From this, I concluded that Christmas would kill me.

Why shouldn't it? It had killed all the others, that was a matter of Statistics, and what right had I to be spared? Particularly considering how I'd begun to feel about it. Year after year, the same ebbing of spirit, the tug of gravity every time I heard a Salvation Army bell, the malaise of dragging up old construction-paper ornaments from the bottom of the ornament box.

The Christmas blahs, that's what my mother would have called them, but that phrase didn't get to the mortality that lay behind them. Christmas walked hand in hand with

Death. Death was there in the boas of tree tinsel and the bestselling thriller that Great-Aunt Alice sent us every year (with the price clipped off the front flap) and in every cup of hot cider and every Perry Como special and in the jangle of every strip-mall carol. Death lay behind all of it.

And so, as I contemplated the onrushing Christmas of 1978, I felt myself to be standing at the heart of a very busy interchange, with direly accelerating Statistics converging on me, and no other result but this: my own crumpled body laid out on the pavement.

2. Bette Davis

I should say right now I had no very keen desire to kill my-self, and didn't know anyone who had. For reasons that re-main veiled to me, my notions of suicide were derived from *Dark Victory*, in which Bette Davis does *not* kill herself, is merely afflicted with a silent and fatal illness that will hold off (she is told) until the very final minutes of her life, at which point it will register as a gentle dimming of the lights.

Well, if death could come like that, couldn't suicide? Sweep over you like the distant peal of a Salvation Army bell? One minute you're yacking with Geraldine Fitzgerald in the garden; next minute, you're stiff-upper-lipping George Brent out the door and lying down with the shadows.

This left me in a state of halfhearted vigilance, for it seemed to me that at any moment—shopping for tchotchkes at Spencer Gifts, shaking the dead needles from a Jaycees spruce—Death might come whispering in my ear. I had no choice but to arm myself in the manner of medieval saints resisting Satan's thrall: with meditation and self-mastery and, above all, with hard seeds of infrangible wisdom.

3. Glossies

But where was wisdom to be found in the three-bedroom Springfield, Virginia, tract-house-with-carport that was my holding pen? My father had an old King James Bible, but I'd given up on Christianity after two years of attending a wood-paneled Wesleyan chapel called, oh, Something Tum-tum-diddy in the Valley. As for *other* books, well, most of the volumes on our shelves were titles my mother had forgotten to cancel from the Book-of-the-Month Club. Titles like *Rule Britannia* and *The Arms of Krupp* and *The Diaries of Joseph Goebbels*.

And so, by a slow process of elimination, I arrived at the texts that were to be my salvation.

I'm still not sure why we had so many of them. Or why, in a house where disputation was as much a part of dinner as potatoes, these should have been the only journals at our disposal (other than *National Geographic,* an ongoing gift subscription that was stacked, issue after unread issue, in a yellow-rimmed column in my father's basement office). The names, I remember, had a precise allure. *McCall's.*

Ladies' Home Journal. Redbook. Woman's Day. Family Circle. Unabashedly domestic—full of home and hearth and the joy of wax—and yet to my eyes, they were like a portal into another world. A world where "Other Mothers' Milk Kept My Baby Alive" and you could "Cheer Up a Chicken Dinner" with Jell-O apricot salad. A world of "Bags! Bags! Bags!" and needle-lace heirloom bedspreads. A world of faintly ripe fiction ("Wicked Loving Lies") and testaments ("I'll Never Be Fat Again") and, now and then, a touch of condescension ("Your Car: What Makes It Run?"). A world where even the ads seemed to float on tides of mystery: the honey-tressed woman in white peignoir slumbering beneath the words "Shh! Super Plus Tampax tampons at work."

It was a world, more than anything, marked by certainty, and that, for me, was as good as wisdom, if not better.

And I was just in time! Thanksgiving hadn't yet come, and the December mags were already rolling in. Issue after issue, jammed with "*109* Happy Holiday Ideas for the Whole Family" and "*250+* Ideas to Make Your Holidays Merrier." I could make champagne-glass ornaments or tissue-paper garlands, I could paint pillows or sew Christmas bells, and if the holidays were getting me down, I could treat myself to raspberry-leaf tea and a geranium-oil bath.

But I still had no clue about how to survive Christmas until I found, like a sage atop a mountaintop . . .

4. Dr. Wayne Dyer

. . . who, until then, had been nothing more than an occasional guest on the *Dinah!* show. The only thing I could have told you about him, honestly, was that he was bald. And *happy*, yes, I remembered him being happy, but I had decided by then that happiness was no more transmittable than gallstones and that hearing someone tell you how to be happy was like having someone with a double-jointed body tell you how to dislocate your wrist.

But there was no escaping this particular column. No escaping that headline: "Christmas Is for Children . . . Enjoy It Like a Child!" And no escaping the thesis: "In order for you to thoroughly enjoy the upcoming holiday season in the way you once did," wrote Dr. Wayne, "you must reclaim it from the youngsters."

He then proceeded to diagram all the ways in which pure childhood responses are curdled by adult living. A child, wrote Dr. Wayne, would say, "What can I buy to give to Grandma, Billy, my teacher, the neighbors, etc.?" An adult would ask, "Why should I do anything for those people? They aren't important to me." A child would ask, "Do we have to take the tree down already?" An adult would exclaim, "Thank God the holidays are finally over!"

The key, said Dr. Wayne, was to rediscover that lode of childlike joy and wonder, and drive our spades straight into it—to revel with newly minted senses in the lights and decorations, the stores, the people, the gifts. And if we succeeded in overhauling our jaded beings, the big day would once again be The Big Day.

"Yes, Christmas *is* for children," concluded Dr. Wayne Dyer. "The children in all of us!"

5. Show Business

No sooner had I read those words than I remembered the sign I'd seen while emerging empty-pocketed from the video-game arcade: WANTED: TEENAGER, HIGH SCHOOL PREFERRED, TO BE RUDY THE REINDEER! (NO BENEFITS)

I knew Rudy. Knew him well, having seen him any number of times in Christmases past. He lived on the ground floor of Springfield Mall, somewhere between Garfinckel's and Waldenbooks and JCPenney. He was not, strictly speaking, a *whole* reindeer. More like a spotted head and a pair of front legs bursting from a bank of "snow." His head, I remembered, was tilted to one side, as though someone had pistol-whipped him, and he had eyes of black mesh (for concealing the human within), and his nose blinked according to some weird circadian rhythm all its own, the kind that could be decoded only by paranoid schizophrenics.

Rudy, in short, was the best a fledgling mall could do in those days; it didn't matter. That cheap, stunted little half-reindeer had become, in a stroke, the answer to my prayers.

For what better way to reclaim my childhood joy than by bringing joy to children?

Instantly, there grew in my mind the picture of a long line of boys and girls, sparkle-eyed, apple-cheeked, quivering in their parkas. *Are we there yet, Mommy? Can you see Rudy yet?* I would be the cynosure of all their hopes, the fulfillment of their dreams. In the guise of a reindeer, I would give them the happiness they had always wanted, and I would find my own happiness. And Christmas wouldn't kill me.

———◆———

So that's how I ended up in a tiny windowless room in the back of Springfield Mall, being interrogated by a man who had likely tortured Viet Cong. And that's why, when he asked me why I wanted to be Rudy, I vacillated between candor and lies . . . and ended up groping down a middle path, mapless and dangerous.

"I like children," I said, edging my way along. "I really like making them happy. Happy children, that's, personally speaking, what makes me happy."

"Do you have any experience in working with children?" he asked.

"Experience."

"Well, do you have younger siblings, for instance?"

"No."

"Do you tutor?"

"Not . . . not right now, no."

"Maybe you've done some babysitting."

I ran a quick tabulation: Eric Hyde (once), Johnson kids up the street (once); I'd never been asked back.

"Yes," I said slowly. "I have done babysitting. I think you'll find I have excellent references."

He was silent for a moment, making a close study of his cuticles. And then he declared (to nobody in particular): "We usually prefer to hire girls."

"Sorry?"

"Girls, in our experience, have more empathy than boys. Younger children find them more approachable." He leaned forward in his orange chair. He was warming to it now. "You may have noticed this reindeer is called *Rudy*, not Rudolph. We keep his sex as neutral as possible. This enables us to hire either a boy or a girl."

"Well, the thing is," I said. "The point is that, despite being a boy, I've got *loads* of empathy. I'm considered highly empathetic."

"Is that right?"

"People come to me, you know, to talk about their problems. They come to me a lot, which is fine because I'm a *listener.*"

Those frozen-turd eyes got even colder and harder. He was taking my measure down to the scrotum.

"Very well," he said. "We're going to set up a little scenario. Do you know what a scenario is?"

"Yes."

"We're going to pretend a little girl has come to you. She's in distress. She's crying."

"Why is she crying?"

He looked at me as though he hadn't heard me right. "She's crying because she's lost."

"Ah."

"Is that clear? She needs . . . help . . . finding her . . . mother."

"So, in other words, she's not interested in a particular *gift* item. She just wants help."

"Help, that's right," he said. "And you are the only friendly face she can turn to."

"I've got it."

We stared at each other for a good half-minute.

"You can begin," he said dryly.

"Oh, so she's already come up to me?"

"Yes."

"And she's made her situation clear, and now I'm going to respond."

He expelled a long breath through his nostrils. "Yes."

And still I held back. And the longer I stayed silent, the more I felt the air crackle around me.

"Is there a problem, son?"

"No, the thing is I'm just wondering if you want me to speak in my own voice."

He leaned forward, and he said, "Whatever makes you comfortable."

And then came the smile—the smile he had used on the Viet Cong—and I saw in a flash the trap that lay yawning before me. I couldn't speak in a grown-up boy's voice—boys weren't welcome here; and I couldn't summon back the treble of my youth—that was gone for good. And so in the same way I was trying to steer between truth and fantasy, I would now have to find a *voice* that lay in the trackless region *between* boy and girl. A voice that might convincingly emerge from a sex-neutral reindeer in a low-rent mall in a high-density suburb.

I would have to find this voice now.

"Well, hello there, little girl!"

It was a sound I had never heard coming out of myself—or anyone—or anything. High and brittle and vibrato-free and strangely shaggy around the edges and piercingly, damningly unpleasant. It was the kind of voice that could wake up sheep.

"Don't cry! It'll be all right . . ."

It might have been a mercy if he'd laughed. But he sat there with his arms crossed, daring me to go on. And so I did. I went on.

"Tell Rudy. Rudy's got lots of pals back at . . . back at Santa's shop . . ."

The tiniest tingle of sweat then: cold and fugitive, stealing along my hairline.

". . . and they can take care of you, everything's going to be . . ."

A tightness in the chest, a shortness of breath . . . all the signs of a coronary, I thought . . . except for this voice, this Voice, which carried on independent of breath, independent of me.

"*Everything will be all right!*" it shrieked.

And by now, I could no longer look at my interrogator. No, that way lay Death. My eyes scuttled across the room, looking for new attachment points, and not finding any, they scrolled up. And in the ensuing darkness, I tried to call back the acting class I'd taken back in fourth grade, in the Brookfield Plaza strip mall . . . and found that the only thing I could remember was playing an elephant named Tuscaloosa.

This would not do. I would need to channel Lee Strasberg. *What would Lee Strasberg have said?*

Lee Strasberg would have said: Create an image, a sense memory, of this little girl, in the full pitch of her abandonment. Find her in you. Tell me who she is, what she looks like.

She is . . . eight. She has orange hair and dull eyes, and her tears have left furrows along her cheeks, and her chest is heaving . . . inside a . . . a green velvet dress with a red bow and a Peter Pan collar . . .

"*Oh, my, that's a pretty dress you have! What a pretty dress. Hey, what do you say we find your mother? Don't cry, little girl. Don't cry!*"

She was fading as quickly as she had come, and I was now back inside my own symptoms. The trail of snail sweat on my face. The shuddering of lungs. And the sound of my own fingers scratching on my chair like a coffin lid.

*"You just wait right here while I get my . . . magic . . . North Pole phone. Because the North Pole is also a . . . a tele-*phone *pole. And I'm going to call for . . . call for . . ."* I broke off. "Excuse me, does the reindeer come with a telephone?"

He pushed his lips out. He regarded me for a long time. "Walkie-talkie," he said.

"I'll just call up the old walkie-talkie—you know how those work!—and please don't cry 'cause Rudy hates when little girls cry. It makes Rudy want to cry himself. Boo hoo! See, you've got Rudy crying. Boo hoo!"

And now, at last, shorn of breath, shorn of will, the Voice—in all its garishness and nakedness—began to fail.

"We'll find your mother. What does she look like? Is she . . . maybe she's . . . she might have a, you know, a . . ."

And like that, it was gone. No more Voice. No more Hope.

I stared down at my blue jeans. I murmured:

"If you want, I could try another voice."

Which, of course, was the final, the most exquisite humiliation. That after all this, I would still be *begging to be his reindeer.*

He raised himself from his seat. Studied me one last time and then angled his watch toward his face. "Well," he said, suddenly breezy. "Thanks very much for your time. We'll call you if you're still in consideration."

I shook his hand, feeling the hard, knobby carapace of his bones close around my soft, green turtle flesh.

"And if we don't speak again, son, happy holidays."

———————

It wasn't *his* voice, though, following me home. It was The Voice, scalding me with its memory. And, yes, speaking to me, though it would remain forever silent. It was telling me that Dr. Wayne Dyer was wrong. It was saying there *was* no going back—no going forward—only a kind of stumbling in place. That was my best of hope of living through Christmas.

And so, like a sick caribou about to be abandoned to predators, I staggered on against my body's own promptings.

That Christmas, I organized a group of carolers to serenade neighborhood homes. (We scattered after one of our friends' dads stormed out with a gun.) The next Christmas, using a recipe and grid from the *Ladies' Home Journal,* I made a gingerbread house. (It broke so many times that it had to be sheathed in confectioner's glue, over and over again, until it resembled the body cast of a house.) In the coming years, I would bake cookies, make macramé snowflakes, attend Anglican midnight services, memorize T. S. Eliot poems, perform anonymous acts of charity . . . I would do many things in the name of surviving Christmas . . . but the one thing I couldn't bring myself to do was confront Rudy the Reindeer.

Whenever I had occasion to visit Springfield Mall, I would travel half a mile to avoid encountering him (her), and if for some reason I couldn't avoid the thing, I would pass by on a current of steam, with my eyes averted.

Only when I was well into my twenties did I feel strong enough to face Rudy straight on. He was much as I remembered him. The head was tipped a little more to the side, the bank of "snow" was grimy with the undersides of Converse All-Stars, and the nose was still carrying on its anemic and fitful blinking—the strange private rhythm that now, as I studied it, assumed a larger meaning.

For it seemed to me that, in the end, there was no better example to follow than Rudy's. There was no better answer to Death's cold, hard stare than this. Flicker our sad little off-kilter lights. Leave Death trying vainly to guess our pattern. Dazzle him with our sheer human incomprehensibility. And in this manner, Death could be, if not defeated, at least blinded, held at bay.

Which was exactly what I'd done, I now realized, not through any system but through a sheer want of system. And it was something of a miracle in its own right that, having spent all that time trying to survive Christmas, I had never stopped to notice the most salient fact: I had survived. Survived gingerbread houses and Dr. Wayne and *Family Circle* and actuarial statistics and Bette Davis. I had even survived Rudy. Here, *here* was my dark victory.

I'LL HAVE CHRISTMAS WITH THE WORKS ON RYE, HOLD THE HAM AND JESUS

Valerie Frankel

———◄►———

The worst Christmas I ever had was the year we celebrated Hanukkah. This was in 1974. I was nine. Our family had just moved from racially diverse, middle-class West Orange, New Jersey, to the affluent suburb of Short Hills. In all fairness, Short Hills did have some diversity. In most parts of town, the people were pure white. In others, they were tanning-bed white. In still others, they were whiter-than-white, i.e., blue.

Steered by a canny real estate agent, my parents bought a house on a long, steep street called Great Hills Road. Later on, when I got to junior high and met kids from other neighborhoods, namely, the St. Rose of Lima Catholics and the über-WASPs of the Short Hills Club, I learned that our hilly section was known as Kike's Peak. We lived about halfway up.

Near the top of the peak, veering half a mile to the left, was Deerfield Elementary School. On my first day of third grade, I instantly grasped that I wasn't in West Orange anymore. The complete absence of black faces was one clue. And when the teacher took attendance, I didn't hear a single name that ended in a vowel (except Shapiro). When she read the list, "Feldstein, Lebersfeld, Steinberg, Denberg, Berg. Stein. Feld," I almost laughed. I thought she was making it up. After school, I overheard my mother on the phone describing our new neighborhood as "a Jewish ghetto." Perhaps it was the only ghetto in America where the moms wore mink coats and drove Mercedes-Benz station wagons.

In West Orange, with its mixed bucket of Italians, blacks, Jews, Hispanics, I wasn't aware of being a member of any race or religion. In Short Hills, with its wall-to-wall Jews, I was suddenly self-conscious and confused. I knew I was Jewish, but my religious identity was muddled by my nonobservant upbringing. We were Jews who broke the rules. We celebrated Christmas. And we did it right, throwing a party, the grown-ups laughing and drinking, the kids loading too much tinsel on the trees. I got to wear a brand-new velvet dress, white tights, and black patent-leather Mary Janes. One of the West Orange dads dressed up as Santa, and gave out little gifts like PEZ dispensers, Kiddles, and MatchBox cars. In old photos of those days, my sister, brother, and I are standing in front of a heavily laden tree, mad grins on our round faces.

I associated Christmas with family, friends, presents, food, fun—the same things Gentile America thrills to in anticipation of the holiday. My family (on both sides) had been celebrating Christmas with a feast and a tree for three generations. We did not go to church for Midnight Mass, carol about "Holy Night," hang wreaths, stage nativity scenes, burn myrrh incense. Certainly, we never basted a ham. (Not that we were kosher—even nonobservant Jews have an innate aversion to ham.) As Americans, we enjoyed the secular aspects: Santa, Rudolph, Frosty, sugar cookies, a tree in the living room, opening presents in pajamas, emergency runs to 7-Eleven for batteries.

My happy, cider-scented Christmas associations would fall under a dark cloud in 1974. For the first time, I would be forced to face the truth about the holiday and to readjust everything I'd previously thought. As of that year, Christmas lost its innocence, and took on a frightening new meaning:

The Birth of the Baby Jesus.

In a way, Jews view Christmas with more religious zeal than most (non-Evangelical) Christians. None of my Gentile friends puts Jesus at the center of their holiday swirl. They talk about cooking for twenty, five cartloads at Target, massive Visa bills, flying to Toledo. When asked about the once-a-year golden opportunity to worship their Lord and Savior, they roll their eyes. If all goes according to plan, maybe they can squeeze in five minutes for Jesus between forcing fruitcake on the Labrador, polishing the good silver, and guzzling gallons of eggnog. Christmas for Gentiles can mean a million different things. For Jews, it's all Jesus, all the time.

———————

"Which temple are you going to join?"

"Are you Reformed or Conservative?"

"Have you set a date for your older daughter's Bat Mitzvah?"

Alison, my sister, was in fifth grade and eleven years old. But this was, apparently, way too late for her to have any hope of having a Bat Mitzvah in a "good place," as the Short Hillites informed my parents. Mom and Dad were advised to get their *tukases* in gear if they wanted to lock in a date for me and my seven-year-old brother, Jon.

My mom insists now that social pressure was not the reason my parents decided to join a temple, B'nai ____ (Reformed). Nor was it the horrified reactions of neighbors when we casually mentioned our shady past of celebrated Christmas. The reason for joining, as Mom and Dad explained to us at the time, was ripe opportunity. In the spirit of fresh starts and due diligence, my parents were going to give us what their parents had failed to give them—a formal Jewish education. That meant Hebrew school on the weekends and observing major Jewish holidays.

Hanukkah was the first up after joining the temple. De-

spite my parents' commitment to the Semitic cause, they re-
mained clueless about how to observe, and they certainly
weren't going to ask the judgmental new neighbors for tips.
My mother had only a vague idea of what to do that first
night of Hanukkah. We didn't have a menorah, so Mom tore
eight holes in a kitchen sponge and filled them with pink
birthday cake candles. She lit all eight candles at once, and
we watched them burn down to the sponge. Mom threw the
singed yellow rectangle into the sink and rinsed it in cold
water. Then she handed out wrapped presents to the kids.
My sister, brother, and I each got a six-pack of tube socks.

Disappointment is a severely underrated emotion. And it
didn't begin to address our concern that a burnt sponge
and tube socks were replacing our beloved Christmas. "So
what if Christmas was the day Christ was born?" we cried.
"Jesus was a Jew!" we stated repeatedly. It went on like this
for eight crazy nights. Meanwhile, the Gentile world was
spinning into a frenzy of joy at the coming of Christmas. I
despised our self-imposed sanctions, and felt a bit of Jewish
guilt for hating Hanukkah by comparison. The resentment
increased daily.

And then, a glimmer of hope. A few days before Christmas, Dad announced, "We made plans for a ski trip. We
leave on Christmas Eve."

My sister, brother, and I rejoiced! We were to escape the
oppression of exclusion! As it turned out, we weren't original with this strategy. The traditional Jewish activity of

choice on Christmas—besides dinner at Kung Fu Palace
and a movie—was travel. Since the goyim were home con-
suming pork and cocktails on Christmas Eve and Day, the
Jews of Short Hills took to the empty skies, venturing to
Florida, the Bahamas, Mexico. The Gentiles could have
the Virgin Mary. The Jews would take the Virgin Islands.

My dad had always been a devout skier, and since we
were way too late to make a reservation anywhere south of
Short Hills, we were to head north, to Sugarloaf, in Maine.

We drove. Even at nine years old, I realized my parents
were crazy to attempt it. Five people, several suitcases, and
loads of ski equipment made for a cramped wagon. I had
terrible car sickness, and we had to stop so I could vomit
on the side of the highway. My brother squirmed and
hummed annoyingly. My sister's severe adult claustropho-
bia is probably rooted in that drive. We stopped in
Portsmouth, the last outpost in New Hampshire, for dinner. The waitress brought our lobster rolls, and my mother
said, "Hooray! We're on the border of Maine!" We'd been
on the road six hours already.

Dad said, "Halfway there!"

My sister sobbed.

My brother hummed.

I threw up.

Hours and hours later, when we got to Sugarloaf, we saw
why last-minute reservations were possible. The ski lodge
was still under construction. The residential condos were

only partially wired for electricity. Our two rooms—meaning, a living room/bedroom and a bathroom—didn't have
reliable heat. The good news, my dad told us when we
checked in, was that the mountain had three feet of fresh
powder and that the skiing would be excellent. Good news
for him. We kids were only four feet tall.

We never set ski to slope, anyway. The next day, Christmas, we woke up to the ping of sleet on the roof. From our
condo window, we watched golf ball–size ice nuggets
bounce in the parking lot. It was just as cold inside. Fully
dressed in ski clothes with our hoods up and mittens on,
we asked if we could watch TV. "Sorry," said Mom. "The
room doesn't have one." We asked if we could go to a
movie. The nearest movie theater, or library, or *anything*,
was three hours away. It sank in that we were in the middle
of nowhere with nothing to do in a freezing room on
Christmas. But, Mom said, "We're together."

For Christmas dinner, we went to the ski lodge. We were
the only customers there. The sole person working was a
grumpy middle-aged woman who kept looking at her
watch. We ate the one option on the menu: beef chili with
cheddar cheese. Sitting on plastic chairs at a plastic table
and pointedly ignoring the malevolent stares of the grump,
we ate quietly and quickly. I'm sure each of us was thinking
about the Christmas dinner of the year before: the roast
turkey and stuffing, gravy, cranberry sauce, shrimp cock-
tail, cheese puffs, hot cider with cinnamon, and unlimited

cookies and candy. Mom said, "This is the best beef chili with cheddar I've ever tasted." We would all continue to taste it for days.

Back at the condo, Dad surprised everyone by digging into his suitcase and removing a rolled-up piece of green fabric. He unfurled it and presented a green triangle with colored circles sewn onto it, a brown rectangle on the bottom—a cotton Christmas tree. Dad used the top loop to hang the tree from the closet door.

Alison said, "Dad, that's cheating."

A man of few words, Dad smiled and shrugged.

We laughed with illicit joy at our rebel father and soaked in the smallest symbol of Christmas in our frozen, shoebox-size condo.

Still hoping to get some skiing in, we waited another day for the sleet to stop. It didn't, so we drove home, arriving in Short Hills in the middle of the night. Mom and Dad carried us to bed.

When we woke up and stumbled downstairs the next morning, my sister, brother, and I were shocked to find a pinball machine in the living room. Not an arcade model. About one-third the size, with yellow plastic legs and a colored cardboard playing surface, it had shiny silver balls and moving flippers. It lit up and made beep sounds when a ball hit a bumper (until the batteries died). We loved it. I had no idea when Mom and Dad bought and/or assembled it. We hugged them in gratitude. They stood watching us with mugs of steaming coffee in their hands and weary-yet-relieved expressions on their faces, having managed to pull off Christmas despite the forces of God and man that were standing in the way.

We resumed our Frankel Christmas tradition the following year. Our neighbors and classmates frowned upon it. I started to give people the explanation I continue to recite about thirty times each season: "We're Jews but we celebrate Christmas. For us, it's not about the birth of Jesus, of course. It's a secular, American observance." This explanation didn't fly with the religious leaders at B'nai ____. A letter arrived at our house on temple letterhead. "It has come to our attention that some of you have a Christmas tree in your houses and call it a Hanukkah bush," read the note. "This is unacceptable. Jews cannot celebrate any aspect of Christmas. There's an oil crisis in America, and it is essential to uphold the Jewish traditions and be unified in our actions. All those Gentiles you think are your friends, given the choice between Jews and oil, they'd pick oil."

My mother called up the temple director and said, "If the priest at St. Rose of Lima said at church, 'Given the choice between Catholics and oil, the Jews would pick oil,' you'd have the Anti-Defamation League over there before you could say *Hanukkah* ten times fast." Which, actually, wouldn't be that fast.

The infamous "they'd pick oil" letter thereby ended our association with B'nai ____. My sister, brother, and I never had Bar or Bat mitzvahs, or much of a Jewish education. Dad announced that he would earmark the temple membership fees for a ski vacation each year instead. He kept that promise. And over the years we have skied across the country, from Vermont to Wyoming.

Needless to say, we never went back to Maine.

Now that I'm an adult with (Jewish) children of my own, we celebrate Hanukkah the right way. We say the prayers in Hebrew and English. We light the candles from right to left on a proper menorah. I give small gifts each night at sundown. I make latkes.

We also celebrate the Frankel family secular, American-style Christmas—baking cookies, buying gifts for the extended family to put under the heavily laden tree—at Mom and Dad's house. Sometimes we go to Short Hills, sometimes to their farm in Vermont. Doesn't matter where we are because, as Mom says, "We're together." The family is bigger now. Louder. We still run out for emergency batteries, eat unthinkable amounts of food, and open presents in our pajamas. I watch with a steaming mug of coffee in my hand, a weary-yet-relieved expression on my face. Each year, we retell the story of the pinball machine. It's part of the tradition now. And each year, the adults rejoice, having managed to pull off Christmas again, despite the forces of God and man that are always standing in the way.

CHRISTMAS IN PARIS

Mike Albo

———◆———

While driving me to the train after visiting last Christmas, my Republican but understanding father told me next time I could bring someone home with me. All I could say in response was a cheery "Okay!" while I looked at the Northern Virginian vista of plazas and neo-Colonial homes.

I can't imagine bringing someone home for Christmas. You and your gay partner (what everyone would call him before you two arrived) would have to be groomed like grooms, dressed in carefully fitted American Apparel clothes that didn't look too matchy-matchy, conversing with semi-masculine voices about your career and cars.

If I could jam my byzantine, vague relationships with men into a tightly wrapped gift, I would. My affairs don't fit easily into one seat at the dining room table.

"Hi Mom, hi Dad! This is F. I just met him on Saturday! We made out at the Slide, and then my friend Bill said that he had had sex with him last week and that it was great!"

"Hi Mom, hi Dad! This is R. We hook up occasionally, but then he always ends up talking about his stupid boyfriend in Berlin so I am not allowed to feel anything significant for him!"

"Hi Mom, hi Dad! This is G and S. They are a couple who kind of have sex with me but also have sex with other guys, too!"

———— • ————

When I was thirty, I fell in love with this guy who I had barely had sex with who had an "open relationship" with his boyfriend. Let's call him G. (I would try to make up a full fictional name for him, but right now I can't think of one that doesn't have pre-attached meaning to it. So let's just stick with initials.) He was blond and lunky and had a face on the angelic side of looks. His boyfriend, S, was a sexy, acrobatic, freckly dancer who was often out of town traveling with a dance company. Their apartment was decorated in perfectly shabby chic furniture and items they brought back from their trips to Zimbabwe, Thailand, and Guatemala: headdresses, conch shells, worn-in wooden beads, and chandeliers with oyster interiors. They would walk around their apartment shirtless, hosting parties, and doing tons of drugs that never seemed to affect their toned bodies. They had a dreamy array of friends from their travels and S's dance company tours: A British girl who I found out later was a Lady. A brooding, gorgeous French actor with a promising career. Two angularly handsome, intelligent brothers from Brittany, who insisted, with genuine, un-American sincerity, that I come visit them.

It was 2000, and G lived a rambling, fabulously worldly lifestyle that matched that spotlessly positive year. He seemed to have money from somewhere, and would spend a lot of time on Orbitz or CheapTickets.com finding amazing deals to Mexico, Costa Rica, Los Angeles. We began to take trips together. He would call me up, and in a week I would be on another plane with him and S, to another beach or city or hotel, a Lover Without Borders. Foolishly openhearted, I suppose I was in love with S, too. He seemed welcoming and happy to have me around, and we kissed when we were drunk.

———— • ————

I don't think I really set out to sleep with them, but slowly, over the year, I did, between them—sort of sexually but sort of not, like I was a house cat. I was caressed; they laughed at my jokes and fed me. When S was gone, G gave me more attention, and we would make out. But it was kept above the belt, so it seemed "okay."

I know how completely unhealthy it sounds, but remember, it was 2000, before the paradigm shift, and it seemed right at the time. I think I had a job then, but I just remember buying CDs with G, chatting with him constantly on my new Nokia cell phone, and charging sashimi deluxe dinners for us on my MasterCard, calmly trusting that somehow in the blue, confident glow of our boom economy, all would be easily paid off by day-trading for a couple of hours. I was like an Enron executive of desire, bloated with confidence.

But also like a white-collar criminal; in the back of my mind I knew this idyllic arrangement was doomed. I spent the year with them, in various hotel rooms from Chicago to Zihuatanejo, accruing debt, believing the hype, waiting for a significant moment, I guess, when G would look at me, next to a lakeside landscape or other beautiful, expensively lit location, and tell me, finally, how strongly he felt. Everything would fall in place, and either G would break up with S and devote himself to me, or, even better, the three of us would get married and live a fantastic, slightly Euro life that bent conventions.

G's self-made life made me question the whole "This is my boyfriend!" schematic that kept me feeling inadequately single every Christmas. He was thrilling and made me feel expansive, like the smell of airports. He was an alluring, beckoning, blue-eyed escape.

———— ◆ ————

One night, in early December, G and I were drinking dollar beers ironically at the Dugout, an old West Village gay bar. G also had a little baggie of coke. (Lord knows how I did that drug back then. The next day I would always wake up sick, looking rapidly aged and part lizard, like I was in special-effects makeup.)

G grabbed me by the waist. "I bought you a ticket to Paris for Christmas." We would fly there, spend the night, and then S would join us, coming from Geneva, where he was rehearsing a dance performance. The three of us would travel to Brittany and spend Christmas Eve with the two angularly handsome, intelligent Breton brothers and their parents at their converted farmhouse on the outskirts of Rennes.

I made one feeble gesture of hesitation. "I don't know. My parents would be so disappointed."

Hopped up, G hugged me and bit me on the neck. "Screw your parents." he said. "Let me be your daddy." He followed it up by looking at me with blue eyes that lit up like gas jets. I bent and bent my Prevacid cardboard beer coaster into four fibrous tatters.

Listen, reader, I know I shouldn't have gone. Trust me: years have passed; I have shoveled myself out of debt and acknowledged my faults. In our country it's impossible to do anything rash and passionate without immediately being confronted by all the self-killing therapist-speak floating in the air like soft Muzak: I keep choosing men I can't have. I avoid serious, fortifying relationships in favor of "destructive" ones. I am insecure or narcissistic or obsessive-compulsive or whatever else. I know, I know, I know.

Before you roll your eyes and think I am just a silly, ranting queer, let me ask you: Would YOU have turned down a ticket to Paris for Christmas with a totally hot guy? Ask of yourself, my reader, and then, ye be the judge of me.

———

I was on Flight 929 to Paris, seat 28F, dead center of the airplane. G was to my left. He gave me a Valium and bought us three small bottles of Cabernet. He gazed at the flight attendant, and she gave us an extra bottle. There was such promise in everything around me—in the twinkling seat belt lights and soft, square blankets and rhombus-shaped chicken breasts. An old man sat to my right reading a book entitled *In Quest of Nirvana*—a wink from the universe of what was to come.

We got off the plane, and G knew exactly where to direct our taxi. There was a fresh wind blowing, the mild temperature of a floral refrigerator. G had reserved a hotel room in Montmartre, where buildings sprout out of steep streets and look crooked. We walked past shops, with cheeses and fruits arranged in the window like *Gourmet* magazine covers. Everyone passing by wore their scarves and peacoats with effortless style. Schoolchildren in cute uniforms ran by giggling. I had walked onto the set of my own private *Moulin Rouge*.

Our hotel room was orange and gold. Across the way, a stone church charmingly clanged its bell on the hour.

There were two twin beds. G slid them together to make one, and I felt a Frenchy breeze inside of me. We went to a perfect little restaurant nearby with a rusty spiral staircase up to an airy room where we ate next to an aviary of chirping birds. The staircase was a little hard to negotiate on Valium and red wine, but Paris was so well art-directed, I felt like I didn't need to have much balance. We studied a face-lifted woman sitting next to us as she constantly adjusted her Hermès scarf, and it instantly became another marvelous private joke between us. "You are my favorite person to travel with," G said. Everything was pointing so passionately toward a lovely climax that I felt all I needed to do was be classy and wait for that perfect moment, when G would make some absolute statement.

After dinner we walked through Pigalle and ended up at a dark little bar called Flipflop, near our hotel. We met the friendly owner, Thierry. It was poetry night, and we listened to drunks ranting spoken word in French. G put his arm around me and ordered me three Labats in a row. I drank them, and Paris turned into a nostalgic Impressionist poster. I was enjoying the colorful smears when I saw G talking to Thierry. "He has hash," G told me, and we walked outside.

We were back at the hotel room, with Thierry. There was a short talk about the Future of Art when the Frenchman suddenly dove on G and kissed him. G kissed him back. I watched them chew on each other's mouths. I sat there, drunk, on the edge of the bed and tried to find the right time to join in, like I was jumping into a double-Dutch match. But Thierry kept getting in the way. I pulled away, closed my eyes, and felt the Spins coming on. I ran to the bathroom to throw up the Labat and rhombus chicken breast and clams and white sauce. I heard their wet smackings while I curled up on the floor tile. Why hadn't G kissed me yet? Did he just want hash? It was the night before Christmas Eve.

—•—

S arrived the next afternoon. He walked into the hotel room and looked at the beds pushed together, and I saw his face slightly fold inward. "I'm feeling a little sick, so I'm going to get another room," he said. There was an unwritten agreement with G that I would not mention the Thierry experience, but I wanted to tell S, because he must have sensed the sexuality in the room. I felt like I was being blamed for being sluttier than I was, when, for once, I wasn't. That night, G slept with his back to me, like we were septuagenarians.

The next morning, Christmas Eve day, he woke up and walked out without saying a word. I went down to the *tabac* across the street and sat there at the brass-topped bar drinking cappuccinos and eating almond pastries (the only thing I knew how to order) and trying to figure out why G was being cold to me. When I returned, the two of them were sitting on the bed, detectably cooling from a heated conversation, smoking the hash. They gave some to me, and we took a taxi to the train.

The wind evolved from delightfully bracing into icy, sudden gusts that made you wince. While we waited for the train, hail came. Thousands of mothballs bounced in front of flower shops and newsstands. The clouds outside were brownish black for most of the trip, and by the time we arrived in Rennes the sky had unnoticeably turned into night. In my hash high, I had no idea where I was, except that the rain was hitting the windows as if it were trying to get to me. We walked into an echoey station and were greeted by the Breton brothers and their father, a handsome Sean Connery look-alike in a heather-gray sweater and intelligent reading glasses. He guided us in the darkness to a sleek silver auto. The rain, whipped up in the wind, pelted my face painfully. I leaned down to put my bags in the trunk and slammed my forehead on the sleek, thin, expensive edge of the gleaming sports car.

In the car, I casually touched my forehead. I felt flaps of skin, and a trickle of blood dripped between my eyes. The cut was gushing, but no one seemed that concerned. I didn't dare suggest their taking me to the emergency room; I'd be perceived as an American hypochondriac. I didn't want to be any more of a nuisance than I suddenly felt I was being on this trip. The father gave me a roll of pink toilet paper. I tried to be cheery and comedic while I held a wad of tissue against my gash.

The car took us out, farther and farther into the flat countryside that appeared as an expanse of tar. The brothers pointed out the shadowy facades of five-hundred-year-old churches. We turned onto a bumpy pathway between high mounds of grass. We pulled up in front of a large brown house that seemed warm inside. The mother greeted us sweetly, scooted me inside, and bandaged me up, pinching my wound closed and taping it with gauze. Then we sat down to eat a beautiful feast—oysters, salmon loaf, layered pig, apples from their garden, foie gras, clementines, lots of red wine. The act of eating kicked in the hash again, and I talked energetically and busied my mind listening to the history of Brittany while I studied G and S closely from the other side of the table. They were shoulder to shoulder. S was whispering angrily. He cut the air with his hand and stood up briskly. He said he was sick and needed to sleep. G looked like a reprimanded dog. After a proper amount of time, he followed him upstairs.

I stayed up and talked with the Breton brothers, but I was jealous and felt like crying. Funny how a mind can do that: divide you into a bubbly social being with the ability to ask questions and say, "I know!" while you seethe inside. I went to the bathroom and looked in the mirror. The gauze on my head was taped into a cross. It was Christmas Eve. I had a bloody cross on my forehead on Christmas Eve.

In the morning, I woke up in a warm bed in the upstairs

loft. I had passed out from the food and wine and felt like a stuffed duck. G and S were on the floor beside me. G's arm was around S, and they were sleeping off the hash, Valium, and alcohol, transforming it all into their consistent good looks as if they were vampires. God, I had to get away from them. I walked down the stairs. I needed one moment to be alone. The sweet mother was awake. She took off my bandage and said that my gash was fine and healing. She gave me some coffee and patted my forehead. "Go outside," she said to me, and pushed me out the door. Outside were bumpy green pastures and a canal. The sky was cloudless. The Bretons' garden was stippled with perennials. Next to the doorway was an old blue wheelbarrow, with three kittens tumbling over one another. I walked down a brick pathway walled in by cypress trees, to a view of a pasture on the other side of rusty barbed-wire fence.

Back in Virginia, my family was having another thoughtlessly pleasurable Christmas Day. My niece and nephew, brainwashed from Disney specials and Nickelodeon shows, their little developing consumer fangs exposed, were tearing through the wrapping paper of gift after gift, just as the tactless Americans before them had done, including me. The room was filling with the smell of fresh, fuming Fisher-Price plastic. My mom was getting a lovely sweater or pair of earrings and growing a little tearful, and my dad was throwing presents to my brothers from across the room—"Hurry up and open 'em!" he always says—having a wonderful time, which, I realized just then, has been one of my favorite things to see.

G came up behind me. "Where are the cows?" he said.

"I don't know."

"Watch out. The fence is electric," he said.

I wanted to hurl myself on it and fry into a little blackened, ignored *pomme frite.*

Why the fuck did you bring me here? I wanted to say. But S beat me to the drama. Anything I tried to say now would seem tiring and overly emotional. And anyway, what right did I have? I was just the tossed-around handbag on this trip.

"It would probably get rid of my hangover," I said instead. G put his arms around me from behind. Here was my moment, but I was too overstuffed and hung over from the sumptuous food, rustic beauty, and from G, who made it all unsatisfying. I wanted to sit in the Dugout and yell at him like I was a brave, runny-nosed drug addict who didn't give a shit who heard him. We walked back, and I stopped to watch those helplessly mewling kittens so well placed and perfectly cute, like the little conniving creatures planned it that way.

Back in Montmartre, G and S slept in the other room. I spent the night alone. The wind sounded like it was picking up again. It whistled through the narrow Montmartre alcoves. In the dim light before sunrise, the windows of my room blew open with a violent whistle and the long white curtains actually heaved and billowed in a manner seen only in horror movies. The church began its ominous early-morning gongs. I sat up in bed, gasping. When would this goddamn biblical, overly symbolic imagery end? I was so afraid that I would be surrounded by escalating, momentous intensity for the rest of my life—doomed bells, hail and howling wind, trees struck by lightning and bursting into flames, infestations of locusts—all with a bloody, weeping mark of Satan on my head!

G walked in at nine and told me, in the flat tone of an itinerary, to hurry and pack and meet him in the *tabac*. Our plane was leaving in three hours. He was cold again. S had already gone back to Geneva, so I guess he didn't need to dangle his seduction over me to keep us both in place. The clouds outside were moving at a threatening angle, as fast as black migrating birds. Warped sheets of metal and shutters from the Parisian windows were strewn all over the streets. I walked with my bags across to the *tabac*, pelted with wrappers, onion skins, leaves, and all the other attractive debris of Paris.

Later, on the plane back to New York, finally reading the London *Independent*, I discovered that deadly high winds had hit France that week—the worst in one hundred years. They'd even blown out the windows of Notre Dame. Something like sixty people had been killed.

At Charles de Gaulle, no one seemed to notice the

scabbed gash on my forehead. Our plane somehow slipped between the storms and ascended before they shut down the airport. It was an empty flight, and G scooted into a seat a row behind me. He took two more Valium and ignored me. With a puckered Charles Manson mark on my forehead, I watched Julia Roberts being a runaway bride on the seatback screen.

I would love to say that all this has been composed with that calm, practiced distance they teach in writers' workshops, and that I am happily coupled now with a nice, supportive hedge fund analyst, and that our clean, supermodern apartment will be featured in the March issue of *Dwell*. Wrong!

I mean, my cut healed; I don't have a satanic scar. Also, I gained, finally, the self-preserving sense to step away from G and S. Although that wouldn't happen for another several months. Upon landing in JFK, I still had yet to experience more fully the rotten undersides that come with being an enchanted fool. I'll spare you the details, but let's just say the drama widened to B, Q, P, R, and F. Know this, reader: I am no longer the junkie mistletoe hanging between two men, but I still have a gusty love that has no home.

I'll be going down to Virginia for the holidays, loving it when absolutely nothing extraordinary happens. I will celebrate a Christmas of scrutable, easy-to-process magic, bought in stores or online. My future husband better fucking appreciate it. Or my two husbands.

WE REALLY MUST GET TOGETHER THIS YEAR

Marian Keyes

———◆———

*I*t's not that I hate Christmas—it being the season of unlimited chocolate, how could I? And, of course, the presents are nice. Not to mention the trifle on Christmas Day. And it's always cheery to see over-refreshed businessmen wearing big, mad, red antlers, swaying on the train home, oblivious to their headgear.

But, as my mother (devout churchgoer) often reminds me, Christmas isn't just about selection boxes and shower gel/body lotion sets of Tresor. No indeed, she's absolutely right; Christmas is about hard, bloody work.

I'm not even talking about having to get up before dawn on the big day to stuff turkeys and peel eight thousand potatoes. (Due to an excellent arrangement I have with my mother, we are both in denial about my being an adult. She's the mother, she does the cooking and she has never actually eaten something I've made. Never. Mind you, most people wouldn't.)

No. What kills me about Christmas is having to send cards. What is it about this particular task that makes me want to end my life? Sadness that there are so many people I don't see anymore? To my shame, it's more like the sheer life-sapping tedium of it all. Especially when people have long addresses. (The worst offenders are those with house names—Traveller's Rest, Formentura Revisited, etc. It's just a waste! A waste of ink, a waste of space, and a waste of an extra ten precious seconds of my time!)

I consider my list, an accumulation of dozens and dozens of people whom I think of fondly but haven't seen for fifteen years and no longer have anything in common with, and a terrible lassitude overtakes me. I wish for a small but harmless domestic explosion, anything to get out of doing it. I could explain next year. "Sorry I sent no card last year, but our clothes horse blew up. We were picking knickers off the hedges well into the new year!"

Then there's the challenge of trying to remember the names of people's partners. If they're still with them, that is. Because, although I might be dying to ask, "Are you still with that weird bloke with the rabbit fixation and the beard that looks like pubic hair?" I just can't. I'm supposed to know. And what if they've had children? A vague half memory surfaces of being sent a photo of a squashed-looking newborn, along with a card saying, "The world welcomes baby Agatha." Or was it baby Tariq? Or—Christ!—was it a dog this lot got? However, in such murky circumstances,

I've found that a catchall "Hope you and the gang are well" usually suffices.

Far trickier is getting the tone right—to convey a message of warmhearted goodwill so that when they open the card they'll smile and say, "Aww look, one from Marian. Isn't she lovely?" BUT—and it's a very big "but"—without being so pally that they'll spontaneously lift the phone and arrange a night out after not having seen me for over a decade.

And so I get to thinking guiltily, this year, would it be so bad if I didn't . . . ? Who'd miss a card from me when everyone gets so many?

And that's it! The decision is made! With a light heart I tell Himself, "I'm not sending Christmas cards this year. Life is too short."

"Fine," he says. "You've enough on your plate." I study him carefully to see if he's being sarcastic, and I can't be sure, so I go away. Which is when I start thinking, But I really like so-and-so. I want to stay in touch with her, not actually to *see* her of course, but I wouldn't like us to lose touch. But if I send one to her and don't send one to her sister, then her sister will think I've snubbed her, which of course I will have, but I wouldn't like her to think I had . . .

The house is filled with Himself's non-reproachfulness. Just because he's sitting at a table methodically inscribing cards to everyone he's ever met doesn't mean he's judging me for not sending any. Nevertheless, my guilt builds and builds.

Some people get around the hell of card-writing by sending what they insist on calling a "round-robin letter," typed in fake-handwritten text. These letters usually begin, "Hello, valued friend." Or, rather, *"Hello, valued friend."* And then the writer tells you about all the fabulous things they've done over the past year, with a load of people you've never heard of. "Back in June, Lacey, Cain, and I did a Jin Shin Jyutsu workshop! We're still walking funny!" And I'm thinking, "Who's Lacey? Who's Cain? What's Jin Shin Jyutsu?"

These letters always end with something like *"Love, light, and blessings to your loved ones and you,"* the subtext being, "Whoever the hell you are."

Obviously, it's an idea . . . I could knock something up on the computer, lash out a hundred copies, and send them off. Mind you, I'd still have to write the bloody envelopes, never having mastered the printed label thing. That still wouldn't get around the long address, Traveller's Rest–type problem.

Anyway, they're kind of creepy and too impersonal and . . . and . . . *American*. Despite my objection to doing Christmas cards, I still prefer to handwrite a personal message. Even if it's the same one on each card. Even if it's always, "We really"—with the *really* underlined—"must get together *this* year."

Then the post yields up the first card of the season, saying "We really"—with the *really* underlined—"must get together *this* year." And I like the person it's from—although not enough to see them, of course—so I think, I'll just send one back to them. Then the next day, five cards arrive, and I'm fond of these people, too, so I dash off five "Really"— with the *really* underlined—"must get together *this* year"s. And then I'm thinking of all the people I haven't sent cards to, and the torment is bad. And anyway, the next day the post brings an avalanche of "We really must get together *this* year"s, and I buckle.

I walk into the room where Himself is sitting, innocently watching telly or whatever, and yell at him, "OKAY THEN, I'LL WRITE THE BLOODY THINGS. HAPPY NOW?"

THE GIFT OF THE MAGI REDUX

Binnie Kirshenbaum

———◆——

*S*ome things to know: Yes, I am Jewish, and therefore it is fair to say that I have no business celebrating Christmas in the first place, but my mother's counter to that comment was always "We celebrate Thanksgiving and we're not Pilgrims." And, as is often the way with converts and infidels, we celebrated Christmas with all the hoopla as if we were to the manger born. True, there was no mention, or display, of this being a religious holiday. It was about Santa Claus and elves and stockings hung by the fireplace and good cheer and a big dinner and sugar cookies and gifts, gifts, and more gifts.

As little ones, we visited Santa at Macy's, to make our requests, and then wrote that very same Santa a letter reiterating our ferocious greed, just so he wouldn't forget. When we got older, we skipped the visit to Macy's, but we still wrote out our Wish Lists.

My mother had very definite ideas about Wish Lists, that the operative word was *wish*; that gifts, all gifts, not just

those at Christmas but especially those at Christmas, were
to be things you wished for. Gifts were things you would
not, or could not, buy for yourself. They were to be luxu-
ries. Special things. Treats. No one in my family ever got
flannel pajamas for Christmas or anything from L.L.Bean.

This suited me just fine. I was, am, then and always,
something of a girly-girl, and Christmas indulged me with
jewelry, pretty scarves, baubles, perfume. That, coupled
with the fact that I devour books as if they were bonbons
(and for many years, hardcover books were as much of a
luxury as silk underpants), I have always considered myself
an easy person for whom to buy a gift.

It was going to be my first Christmas in my own apartment in New York, which was bound to be more magical
than any other Christmas because I was living in New York,
in my own apartment in Greenwich Village, and I was in
love, and possibilities seemed endless, and life, I thought
then, didn't get much better than this.

As an aspiring writer but working waitress, I was without much money. It was the kind of poor that has nothing
to do with poverty. Not real poverty. Ours, my friends'
and mine, was the sort of poverty that hopeful but as-yet-
unsuccessful young artists and writers and actors embraced, because to us, it had, unlike real poverty, a
decided aura of romance, a patina of hip. Also, we knew
it was likely to be temporary. It was the kind of poor that
had us shopping in thrift stores (which I probably

would've done even if I'd had more money because it was the cool thing to do then). I did my laundry in the bathtub and hung my clothes to dry over the radiator. To get out stubborn wrinkles, I boiled water and held the fabric tautly over the steam. I cooked rice and beans and macaroni-and-cheese and my friends and I went to Chinatown for dinners out and we met up in dive bars where we could get a pint of beer for a dollar.

Flashback to the previous August: Michael, my actor/bike messenger boyfriend, and I were walking along Greenwich Avenue, where we paused at a leather goods store to admire the jacket in the window. Even without touching it, I knew it was the softest of leathers. It was black. It had style, a James Dean kind of style. "That's nice," I said.

"Yeah," he agreed. "But I have a leather jacket."

His leather jacket was a brown bomber jacket, old and cracked, and it was okay, functional, but nothing like this.

"Come on," I said. "Let's go in and you can try it on. Just for fun."

He did look pretty damn fabulous in it, and just as he was taking if off, I thought I saw a wistfulness cross his face, which made me think something that I quickly dismissed: He wasn't going to make it as an actor. A couple more years as a bike messenger, his eight-by-ten glossy in his bag, going to auditions between runs, and then what? Sales? His father's business, which had something to do with installing plumbing? I knew then that I was going to buy him this jacket. I made note of the size, and the next day I returned alone to the store and made arrangements for a layaway plan.

Every Wednesday, I dropped off the money I'd managed to save that week through insignificant sacrifices—nothing like cutting off my hair to sell it to buy him a watch fob only to have him pawn his watch to buy me combs for my hair—but sacrifices nonetheless: generic shampoo, no to breakfast out, using the library more than the bookstore. And every time I denied myself a little pleasure, I'd think about his face when he unwrapped the jacket, how happy he'd be.

The week before Christmas, I was all paid up. I took the jacket home and, just to be sure he'd be entirely surprised, I put it in a carton I had gotten from the liquor store. This way, he'd never guess what was inside.

Surely I will not say that in the joy of giving, I gave no thought to the joy of receiving. At the onset of the holiday season, when dusk came in the late afternoon, Michael and I, holding hands, would walk the narrow streets of Greenwich Village, which was nowhere near as posh then as it is now. Still there were plenty of cute shops, and we'd pause at window displays. There was one shop, antique jewelry, on Bleeker Street where I never saw anything I didn't like. And I often said as much. I'd say, "There isn't one thing in this store I don't like." I pointed out, in particular, a cameo brooch, a silver bracelet ornately engraved, a Victorian locket. My hints were anything but subtle. From mid-November until the week before Christmas, I must've pressed my nose to the glass of that shop twenty-five times, each time finding something that caused me to gasp.

Four or five days before the twenty-fifth, on a freezing night, our breath making puffs of cold, Michael and I, having decided we would have Christmas at my apartment as opposed to his uptown, walked to Hudson Street, near Jane. There we bought our tree from one of the tree farmers who come to the city each year, bringing the smell of pine with them, along with old-fashioned holiday spirit. We could not afford a big tree, a full tree, so we chose a scrawny one, sparsely limbed, half bald. As if a cut-down tree had feelings, we projected this one's need to be wanted, as if going unsold would make it cry.

Half of the few needles it had to begin with were lost by the time we got it up the three flights of stairs to my place. We set the tree up by the window (minor arguments ensued about getting the damn thing to stay upright in the stand) and decorated it with found objects: ribbons tied into bows, bits of pretty paper, small toys, earrings that had lost their mates. It was so sweet as to be treacly, as it should have been.

The next day, I put the gaily wrapped carton under the tree.

On the twenty-fourth, we didn't get a white Christmas, but a wet one. It rained, a cold rain mixed with sleet, and it went on all day while I prepared lasagne for our Christmas Eve dinner. I layered pasta, cheese, sauce, pasta, and so on, and it was still raining hard when I put the lasagne in the oven.

Michael showed up around five with a jug of Chianti—oenophiles we were not—a loaf of bread, his gift for me, which he put under the tree alongside mine for him, and an old album of Bing Crosby's *Christmas Carol Favorites*. Pure camp, and we laughed ourselves sick over it until we put it on, and then it was just kind of nice.

My gift, that is, Michael's gift to me, was in the shape of a large brick. Not books. And unless he was employing the same ruse I had, an outsize box, it wasn't jewelry. Could it be that burgundy velvet scarf with the silk fringe I'd carried on about? That was my best guess.

So we drank Chianti, messed around a little, drank more Chianti, and while Bing was dreaming of a white Christmas for the fifth time or so, we decided we'd open our gifts before dinner. We were too excited to wait.

"You first." I pushed the carton toward him as if it were really heavy. Slowly and deliberately, he unwrapped the paper—he should have taken that kind of time undressing me, but that wasn't a generous thing to think on Christmas—and opened the carton.

He held up the jacket. His face was entirely devoid of expression, which wasn't exactly the way I'd pictured his response, but I assumed he was stunned. He rested the jacket on his lap and finally he spoke. "You shouldn't have done this," he said. It was his tone. Not the "You shouldn't have done this because it was so unbelievably nice of you, so generous, and what have I done to deserve you?" but rather it was the "You shouldn't have done this" as in "You've made a mistake."

"But you fell in love with that jacket," I said. "You looked gorgeous in it. I wanted you to have it."

"First," he said. "I didn't fall in love with it. You did. Even if it did look good, I didn't want it."

"I saved. Since August. I was saving. Every week." I was hurt enough to be incoherent, hurt enough that I wasn't even angry. Just really, really disappointed, and then all I could say was, "You can bring it back. I have the receipt."

He nodded, tried to smooth things over by saying, "I appreciate the thought. Really. It was a very sweet thing for you to do. It's just that, well, I won't wear it."

I scrutinized him in a way that before I had not: his ratty sweater; the ratty part I had no problem with, but it was ratty acrylic, and it wasn't a cool sweater or anything. I held my tongue and put the bruised feelings aside as he passed his gift to me.

It wasn't just shaped like a brick; it was as heavy as one, too. I shook it. Nothing.

And then I tore away the paper to reveal a box that read: Panasonic. Automatic Shut-Off. An iron. An iron for ironing clothes. "You got me an iron," I said. Calmly, I said, "You got me an iron."

"Not just any iron. This is like the Cadillac of irons." He reached over and took the box from me. "A top-mount temperature control," he read from the box. "Extra-large water window and fabric guide. Nonstick coating. Cord reel. Steam or Dry."

"You got me an iron?" I looked down at myself, at the beaded sweater I was wearing with the black velvet skirt. I was wearing stockings with a garter belt. I had on spike-heel pumps from the 1950s, a time when comfort did not take precedence over beauty. I had on faux pearl–and–rhinestone earrings. Rings on five out of ten fingers. And Chanel No. 5 perfume, a birthday gift from my mother, who knew a thing or two about what to give a girl. "You got me an iron?"

"Yeah. You're always saying how you need one. Every time you stand there over a pot of boiling water, you say, 'I really need to get myself an iron.' So I got you one. You said you needed it. A hundred fucking times I heard that, how you needed one."

"I need lots of things. Every month I need tampons. Periodically I need lightbulbs. I need toilet paper. I need shampoo." In the background of our argument, Bing Crosby sang. *Pa rum pum pum pum. Our finest gifts we bring. Pa rum pum pum pum.* "I need toothpaste," I went on. "I need a new dishtowel. I don't want these things as Christmas gifts. Especially not from my boyfriend."

I am a poor boy, too. Pa rum pum pum pum. I have no gift to bring. Ra rum pum pum pum.

"Yeah, well. At least you can use the iron. What am I supposed to do with that jacket?"

Shall I play for you? Pa rum pum pum pum. On my drum.

So he and I both should have felt like a pair of ingrates, spoiled little shits, but it wasn't the iron exactly. "How could you so not get me, who I am?"

"The same way you didn't get me," he said. And then he muttered, "Some fucking greaseball jacket I wouldn't wear if you paid me to."

I stood up and kicked over the Christmas tree.

"What did you do that for? You whack job," he said.

I had no answer really. I did it because I was hurt, because this Christmas was ruined, this one Christmas that was supposed to be magical and was awful instead. "Get out." I stared at the floor.

"You know this is it? It's over," he said.

"I know."

He put on his brown leather bomber jacket, and just as he was halfway out the door, I said, "Michael."

"What?"

What? What was I going to say? I was going to say that the reason I bought him the very hip black leather jacket was because I knew; I knew he'd never make it as an actor; that there was nothing special about him and so I'd wanted to give him something special.

But I couldn't say that. So I just said, "Merry fucking Christmas to you, too."

I left the tree on its side. I left the balled-up wrapping paper, like a pair of red and green tumbleweeds, on the floor, and I poured myself another glass of wine. Hungry now, I took the lasagne from the oven. It had dried to the consistency of taco chips. I tore off a hunk of bread from the loaf, and I went and sat in a chair by the window.

It occurred to me that now might be a good time to cry, but I couldn't quite get myself there. The city was quiet in a way I'd never heard before. The streets were deserted. The rain had stopped, but it had frozen. The trees were coated with ice as if they were made from glass. And I thought, I'm in my own apartment in New York and my life is before me and anything can happen and the trees look as if they are made from glass and this is so fucking great.

On Christmas Day, I did what a lot of Jews do: I ordered in Chinese food, which I ate in bed while reading *The Magic Mountain.* The following day, the twenty-sixth, I took the leather jacket back to the store and exchanged it for a jacket for myself. The twenty-seven dollars I got back along with my new jacket (mine being that much less expensive than his), I gave to the first homeless person I saw. For this I was chastised by a passerby, who said, "You shouldn't give him money. He's only going to buy liquor with it."

"And why shouldn't he?" I asked. "Why shouldn't he get what he wants? Isn't that what Christmas is about? Getting something that you want?"

I'd like to say that the reason I did not return the iron to Michael was because we never saw each other again, which we didn't, but that wasn't the reason. And I could even say I didn't return it to the store because I didn't know where he'd bought it, which is also true. But I kept it because I needed it.

A FOREIGN COUNTRY

Mitchell Symons

———◆———

*T*here's a scene in the 1954 film *The Wild One* where Marlon Brando, playing the prototypical Hell's Angel, is asked what he's rebelling against. "Whaddya got?" he replies.

Well, that's how I feel when I'm asked about hellish holidays and crappy Christmases. Just the one, eh? And how would I go about choosing that? Especially when all those yucky Yuletides merge into one gloomy gloop of ghastliness. Not for me the whimsy of gosh-it-was-so-funny-the-year-we-got-snowed-in or even the pain of the-Christmas-that-Granny-died: both of those are one-offs; my Noels were perennially nasty.

Now, I know that the chances are you're American and therefore accustomed to coming first at everything, even awful Christmases, but I think I can trump just about anything that anyone else could come up with.

You doubt me? Then please consider—in no particular order—the following:

1. The Brussels sprouts we were forced to eat every Christmas Day. These were vicious little creatures masquerading as mini-cabbages but tasting like the devil himself had invented something truly evil just to torment you on the very one day of the year when you needed every one of your digesting skills. And they made you fart.

2. The washing-up. I've seen the films. Just as I know that all American teenagers have their own cars and can always climb out of their bedrooms by using the tree planted for that specific purpose, so I know that ALL American families had dishwashers—oh, and cheesy, smiley moms to fill and empty them. Here in behind-the-times Britain (where, as *you* of course know, we all lived in ramshackle ill-equipped stately homes and couldn't afford orthodontists), dishwashers were a luxury that few families in the cash-strapped sixties could afford. Hence the constant rows as to who was going to do the washing-up. (I know that anyone who's seen British movies will wonder what happened to the butler that *every* family had, but of course he was always given Christmas Day off.)

3. The tacky tinsel and the crappy paper chains and the cheap ersatz decorations that served as a cause of—and a homage to—the cheap sentimentality that surrounds a British Christmas.

4. The film *Miracle on 34th Street*. Yes, I know that you too had to contend with this every bloody Christmas, but consider the following: (a) it's an American film (so you're entitled to it); and (b) during my youth, we had only three—that's right, *three*—television channels, so there wasn't much choice.

5. The Queen's Speech. Irrespective of whether you're a monarchist or a republican (and I tend toward the latter—although I'd happily vote for Her Maj as our elected head of state), there's no doubt that the lady is a born non-communicator. Hell, she can't even communicate with her own children. And her annual televised address to Britain and the Commonwealth—compulsory viewing up and down the land—only serves to cast her subjects into an even greater depression than they would otherwise have been on this most depressing of days.

6. Christmas crackers. Do you have such things? A cardboard tube covered with crepe paper containing a paper hat, a gift, and a joke. The whole thing constructed by impoverished home-workers earning less than a pound an hour. The trouble was that the hat was always too small and it broke as soon as you tried to put it on; the "gift" was something utterly worthless, like a fully nonfunctioning plastic whistle; and the "joke"—in the form of a question that would

inevitably be asked of the whole table—would be as witless as . . . well, judge for yourself: Why do birds fly south in winter? Because it's too far to walk. There was also a thin strip of cardboard running through it with a tiny exploding device in the middle (called, prosaically enough, a "bang"), which was supposed to detonate as the cracker was pulled, but frequently didn't—thereby provoking even more arguments.

7. Socks. If you're an adult male, expect nothing else as a present. And woe betide the man who doesn't manifest surprise and joy on receiving them.

8. The following songs—all of which reached number one at Christmas during my youth: "Long Haired Lover from Liverpool," by Little Jimmy Osmond (a song so incandescently awful that just reading the title will cause the melody to remain in your cerebral cortex for the next three weeks); "When a Child Is Born," by Johnny Mathis (even now that vibrato haunts me); Queen's "Bohemian Rhapsody" (what, if anything, did it all mean, and does it matter very much to me? To me!); "Mary's Boy Child (O My Lord)," by Boney M. (did you get this Stateside? If not, count yourselves lucky—very lucky); and "Mull of Kintyre," by Wings (the Paul McCartney dirge that proved that even great talent needs at least a modicum of taste).

9. Turkey—known in my house as "bloody turkey." Now, look, I know that you chaps all eat turkey on Thanksgiving—and possibly at Christmas, too, but you're not obliged to eat it (in various forms) for seven days afterward. Also, your newspapers aren't full of articles headed, "101 THINGS TO DO WITH TURKEY LEFTOVERS." Yeah, or 102 things if you include eating the damn things.

10. The words *Chrimble* and *Crimbo*—used by shop assistants and the sort of girls who put hearts instead of dots above their letter *i*'s as nicknames for Christmas. I rest my case.

I'm not just riffing: It's hard to overestimate the differences between a British and an American Christmas. If the past is—pace L. P. Hartley—a foreign country where they do things differently, how on earth can I expect to convey *my* past to foreigners? I might as well have come from another planet.

So let me take you to that planet, a place I'll call Christmases in the Sixties and in the Seventies, or CRISIS for short. You'll notice that the acronym's trying too hard (and failing) but, hey, isn't that just a dandy leitmotif for the family Christmases I experienced as a child?

The first thing you should know about CRISIS is that everything's in black and white—or at least that's how I remember it. No, my memory's deceiving me: It wasn't black and white, each of which can be striking and appealing; it was gray (which was even spelt differently on our planet: grey). The weather was sludge grey (I can't remember a single white Christmas), the streets were default grey, and the television—at once, our solitary refuge and our point of congregation—was monotonous grey. Grey is as uncolorful as color can be and yet it was the only color available to us on CRISIS.

The mood too was grey. In between the twin orgies of present-opening and face-stuffing was just nothing. The mood was too anticlimactic to enjoy the presents, and since the Christmas "dinner," invariably eaten between two and three in the afternoon, was several hours away, all one could do was guzzle (*le mot juste*) cheap candy—thus precipitating a series of sugar highs/lows that weren't ameliorated by turning on the TV to see the cheesiest comedian of the day going around the children's ward of a hospital to hand out presents to the kiddies.

Lucky them, I used to think, at least they're spared the misery of a family Christmas, and here, I suppose, is where I must depart from the general and tell you about *my* family's Christmas. For although we inhabited planet CRISIS, we were far from being its only inhabitants, and as Tolstoy wrote in *Anna Karenina* (in fact, it's the very first line), "Happy families are all alike; every unhappy family is unhappy in its own way." Yup, that was us, unhappy in our own unique way.

Funnily enough, the rest of the year we weren't too bad. We were, I guess, no more dysfunctional than any other regularly dysfunctional family. Dad loved all three kids equally but never simultaneously; Mum loved us in descending order—which was okay by me, as I was the middle child between two sisters—but didn't do much for the self-esteem of my younger sister, whose existence I had resented ever since her birth. (When I asked my hitherto omnipotent father to send her back, he explained that it was impossible—hence the "hitherto.") The real fault line in the family was right at the top: Mum wanted a father, and Dad wanted a wife, and we wanted parents who were just like our friends' parents. None of us got what we wanted. Even at the age of six, I knew that that much screaming wasn't normal: "None of my friends' parents behave like this," I'd tell them when I'd summoned up the courage to emerge from underneath the bed (my refuge during their worst altercations). "How do you know what they're like when you're not there?" they'd counter, and I'd be obliged to accept their dubious logic—even though I *knew*. Oh yes, I knew.

Sensing my suspicion, my mum would try to reassure me that their arguments and bickering were somehow *healthy*. "At least everything's out in the open," she'd tell me while I bit my lip, yearning for a family in which some things could be shut away. I didn't know the word *cathartic* but I could understand the implication that, far from heralding a seismic family schism, it was these very rows that meant my parents *wouldn't* divorce (like my friend Jonathan's parents had), with all the stigma that that entailed back then in the grey 1960s.

Letting it all hang out might have worked in late-sixties California, but not on planet CRISIS, where there was no summer of love, just a winter of rancor.

My fear and loathing of their self-expression—self-indulgence—was, in fact, my father's fault. It was he who, in an attempt to turn me into as English a gentleman as it was possible for a Jewish kid from a Jewish suburb to be, sent me at the age of eight to a preparatory school—a private school that prepared you for a public school, which was also a private school. (Confused? You should be.) There I was bullied on three counts: I was Jewish. I was a day boy in a predominantly boarding school (yup, that's the English way: you breed children and then send them off to be cared for by borderline pedophiles and sadists at the very earliest opportunity). And I was clever.

I soon learned that to betray your feelings was a sign of weakness. Lips—especially upper ones—were to be kept as stiff as the collars we wore, and woe betide any boy who allowed his to tremble. Oh yes, I was being turned into a right little gentleman. I even managed to titter along with the rest of the class when Mr. Alston, the dapper little French teacher, told us that the word for cake was *gâteau*— "pronounced 'gatt-oh,' and not as they say in Golders

Green"—a particularly Jewish suburb—"'ghetto.'" How droll, and after all, it was at least twenty-three years since the liberation of Auschwitz.

The truth about my Jewishness was that I was only really aware of it—in the breach as it were—at school. At home, we weren't at all observant—hence our celebration of Christmas (we'd tried Hanukkah one year, but we'd all felt frustrated by the fact that it went on for over eight days without a single day of splurging and so had dropped it)— and since my home friends were all Jewish, it wasn't an issue with them, either.

However, I couldn't help but bring my newfound sensibilities home with me, so that now when my parents started to yell at each other, I wouldn't run away and hide, but would sit there disapprovingly deploring the ethnicity that had undoubtedly provoked their disagreement. For who was I not to universalize my own experiences? My parents argued loudly and they were Jewish; the people at school—the goyim—were (when they weren't beating me up in one of the regular pogroms that triggered any amount of race memory) self-effacing and bottled up. There had to be a connection, and I, who had never heard of a syllogism, duly made it.

The undeniable fact that a lot of the time my parents managed to get on perfectly well—there was always love there, even after they'd divorced (sometime later, when I was in my early twenties)—only served to make their rows worse. I think I could have endured constant antagonism more than the peripatetic bust-ups and love-ins, both of which at once included and excluded me.

Still, what else did I know? And with my elder sister holding the whole family together like some sort of precocious Atlas, we siblings enjoyed as good a childhood as I, with the power of hindsight, could have wished for. Aside from the rows, there was much laughter and fun and warmth. The house was always filled with friends (though not extended family, as my parents conceived a dislike for each other's family), and the summers in particular were halcyon days that I remember with enormous affection. I also recall them in color: the greens of the garden, the blue of the country club swimming pool, and the pinks of the blossoms that lined our suburban street.

As opposed to the grey of Christmas. Over the years, I've given a lot of thought as to why it was so awful, and I've come to the conclusion that the day—the season—acts as a magnifying glass on the emotional health of a family. So if a family is happy, as a family, then Christmas will be especially happy; but if there are (as there were with my family) underlying faults and problems, then Christmas serves to exacerbate them.

So, whereas our family could be perfectly happy at home or, interestingly enough, abroad—the pressures of a family holiday never got to my parents or to us, possibly because my parents were relaxed enough to be able to enjoy themselves and each other and also there was a sense of being united as a family in a foreign country; we might argue among ourselves but we always put on a united front to the world—put us all in the same room at the most miserable time of year (aye, with another three months of winter to come) and we turned into the cast of a Fassbinder movie, albeit without accusing each other of being Nazi murderers. Throw in a widowed grandmother disliked by her son and resented by her daughter-in-law, and you had the perfect recipe for the Christmas from Hell. Or, rather, you didn't have it, WE did.

———— ◆ ————

Have a nice holiday season, won't y'all.

———— ◆ ————

Postscript: Everything turned out fine in the end. I forgave my parents and learned to love my younger sister—though never Christmas. As a husband and father, I took great care to avoid the mistakes of the family in which I grew up—thereby, of course, perpetrating any number of different mistakes. Nevertheless, we almost always go away for Christmas—usually somewhere hot and sunny and . . . and colorful.

THE JEW WHO COOKED A HAM FOR CHRISTMAS

Neal Pollack

———◆———

Nashville, Tennessee, is a very Christian place. You can't go five minutes in December without hearing that damn "Christmas Shoes" song on the radio. So why don't the stores have better food at Christmastime? In December 2004, as my wife, Regina, and I lurched through her mother's neighborhood store, I felt my seasonal joy, never high to begin with, draining away under the gray-dim fluorescent lighting and because I couldn't find any organic peanut butter. It was a perfectly ordinary American supermarket, but I walked the aisles as though it were a crematorium.

Living in Austin, Texas, has spoiled me. The grocery stores are so good that people from Europe visit to study them. On its worst day, my neighborhood store has sixty different varieties of citrus. I've purchased three kinds of bleu cheese made by the Amish in Iowa. My two-year-old son asks to snack on peanut butter–flavored yogurt pretzels. His favorite food, other than ice cream, is capers. And we don't spend any more money than we would at a regular store.

As I walked around that non-Yuppie grocery store, my nose crinkled in disdain. My mouth curled into a sneer usually reserved for people who wear baseball caps backward.

"This is horrible," I said.

"It's not that bad," Regina said.

"How many different kinds of cereal can people actually eat?"

"Yes, dear."

"Why do they call this a grocery store?"

"Because," she said, "this *is* a grocery store."

We arrived at protein alley. The fish looked like it had been in the deep freeze since June. I chose some tilapia for that night, December 23; I could render it inoffensive with tomatoes, garlic, and parsley. The beef, however, looked slimy, with a slight greenish tint beneath the wrapping. I nearly gagged at the sense memory of the sour-sweet smell that red meat gives off just as it's going bad.

"Look at this chicken," I said. "It's all . . . *muscle.*"

Then I saw my dream food, enveloped in a golden glow. A sweet chorus of angels drowned out the tinny Christmas carol Muzak. It sat there alone on the shelf, the last survivor of its kind, in a light-brown burlap bag tied with a little metal ring.

A Smithfield ham.

I'd been dying to eat a Smithfield ever since I read an essay by Southern culinary historian John Egerton in which he called country ham "an ancient and inimitable treasure, the highest form of the Southern gastronomic art." The only thing I coveted more than a Smithfield was a ham from Trigg County, Kentucky. I'd even briefly considered buying a Trigg off the Internet. After all, the mail-order turducken had been a big success two years before. But it was obvious that this Smithfield ham and I were destiny.

"That's our dinner," I said to Regina. "Glory be!"

"Are you sure you want to spend forty dollars?" she said. "It's awfully big."

I looked at her indignantly. "Woman," I said. "Don't you understand? I've longed to prepare a Smithfield ham my entire adult life."

I picked up my ham up and cradled it. The bony back end poked me in the ribs. I bent down and gave it a kiss.

"I love this ham!" I said.

"You're frightening me," Regina said.

"Do you see anyone else volunteering to make dinner this year?"

"No," she said. "But that's because . . ."

My mother-in-law had just moved into a new house and she couldn't figure out how to use the stove. My brother and sister in-law, usually reliable cooks, were bunkered down with a new baby. Regina, as was typical for the holidays, had buttoned up her personality tighter than a Salvation Army sergeant's jacket. The duty fell to me, and just like Mary in the manger, by God, I was going to deliver!

This cheery thought, along with a soap opera magazine, buoyed me all the way through the interminable checkout line. The grumbling clerk ran my items through the scanner without enthusiasm. I got nervous. Did she think I was a Yuppie? Did she resent my forty-dollar porcine baby? I had to prove that I sympathized with her hard life as a working-class Christian, trapped in an awful job in an ordinary neighborhood in a more or less lame city.

"Gosh, I got a really big ham!" I said.

"Uh-huh," she said.

"When I saw that Smithfield ham, I just had to have it!"

"Uh-huh."

"Well," I said. "Happy Holidays to you!"

"I hate it when people say Happy Holidays," she said. "It's anti-Christian. You say, 'Merry Christmas.'"

I looked back at the other people in line. Surely they would mock the provincial attitudes of this foolish woman. No one put up with this kind of crap where I lived. But then I remembered where I was. They all stood there, dour and disapproving. A thin film of menace enveloped the line.

Here's what I thought: You people belong to a majority religion in a right-wing theocracy, yet loudmouthed jackasses have somehow persuaded you that you're some kind of oppressed class! Meanwhile, the government you love is collapsing the economy on purpose. You're all idiots!

Here's what I said: "Heh."

Here's what I should have said: "Yeah? Well, screw you, bitch! This year, Christmas belongs to me! I'm a Jew! And I'm gonna cook a ham!"

———————

Regina's father used to make Christmas the stage for his own personal Southern Gothic Christ-figure melodrama. He was a Catholic by birth only and avoided church like Nosferatu. Nevertheless, a few days before the holiday, he'd dramatically proclaim that no one in his family appreciated him and he'd storm out of the house in a fit. Regina says he would check into a hotel, volunteer at a homeless shelter, and then return home on Christmas Eve day with a car full of lavish presents, pretending that nothing had occurred. This happened almost every year, she says.

In the late eighties, he hit a lode in the risk-management business and began throwing holiday parties at his country club. These parties featured, at one time or another, operettas, vaudeville shows, and Chet Atkins. There were the inevitable ice sculptures, sumptuous dessert buffets to rival anything at the Four Seasons, and thousands upon thousands of dollars' worth of French wine. Several years before he died, he opened a restaurant, which quickly became the only five-diamond establishment in the state. He invited so many people to his final holiday party, which he held at the restaurant, that the party had to be held over three days. In January 1996, his liver gave out.

He'd been gone almost two years when I made my first trip to Regina's family's house for Christmas, in 1997, but this was the South, so his ghost hovered over the proceedings that year like a supporting character in a mid-era Tennessee Williams play. By then, Regina's mother had regained control of Christmas. She was a pious Presbyterian, though not born again and not pushy. The only book in the house I could find, other than the Bible and a volume of cat jokes, was Barbara Mandrell's autobiography. I had more in common with a Bantu elder. The party was over.

Regina's dad had bought a player piano during the 1980s, when every mall had a store that sold them. This one operated via hard disks inserted into a panel on the left side, a technology that was outdated then but now seems as distant as the passenger pigeon. Regina claimed that her mother owned a variety of music for the piano, but she could have had *The Decline of Western Civilization Part One* soundtrack for all I knew. I got to hear only the Christmas disc.

The piano emitted a tinkly moan, playing a song at about one-third its normal speed.

"What the hell is that?" I said to Regina.

"'Away in a Manger,'" Regina said. "Don't you recognize it?"

I didn't, and I could barely make out "The Little Drummer Boy." "Silent Night" seemed more familiar, but the player piano's version sounded like a *Twilight Zone* episode. I imagined a music box turned on its side, playing the same tune over and over again while an old woman shivered in a corner, waiting for death to take her away. Meanwhile, my mother-in-law hummed away cheerfully, dusting the mantel.

"Regina," I said. "How can you . . . stand it?"

"Because it's Christmas!" she said.

The next morning, I came up the stairs to the unbearable racket of a thousand white people backed by an organ. Regina's mother, apparently, had one CD that she played on Christmas when she got tired of the player piano. I've never seen the cover, but if the group doesn't call itself The Worst Church Choir in the World, they're lying. The house shook:

"Noel, Noel, Noel, No-ellllllllllllllll!"

I had to get out of there.

That night, Regina's brother and sister-in-law came over for dinner. We sat around a big-screen TV and watched a video of Dad playing Santa on his last Christmas. I slumped so deep in my chair that my butt almost touched the floor.

"There he is!" Regina's mother said.

"Aww," Regina said. "I see him."

I reached for the champagne and refilled my glass. Regina's father had left behind a wine cellar of high quality. Before I'd popped the first appetizer in my mouth, I must have drunk six glasses from six different bottles. That's about how many drinks it takes, I learned, for a Protestant family to lower its inhibitions. It was a little much for me on an empty stomach.

I ran for the bathroom and bent over the toilet, making a noise along the lines of: "Bleeeeeeeeeeeech. EEEEEEK! URRRRRGH! AAARRRRR!"

After five minutes of this racket, I emerged. Regina's family looked extremely concerned. I reassured them. "No big deal," I said. "I thought I was going to throw up, but I didn't."

A Jew had joined the family.

Over the years, a pattern developed. I would say or do something horribly obnoxious and offensive to Regina's mother. Regina's brother, Brett, who'd been a fullback at Auburn until he'd blown out his knee, would make a comment or two demeaning my manhood. My mother-in-law would get mad at Brett for accidentally dropping something down the garbage disposal. And the painted ponies went up and down. Though I cared about Christmas about as much as I cared about water polo, I wanted to show my new family that I could adapt.

By 2004, Regina and I had been married four and a half

years. I was the father of a toddler. By degrees, I'd become a man. And on Christmas, a man cooks his ham.

I took my ham out of its bag as soon as I got it back to the house. It was majestic, but also kind of disturbing. I'd expected something bright pink that was ready for immediate consumption. This thing looked like it had just been unearthed in an archeological dig.

"There's a lot of fat," I said.

Regina, who'd been dealing with hams her whole life, shook her head.

Smithfields were very salty, or so I'd read. I filled the kitchen sink with water. Gingerly, I lowered my prize and went upstairs to hide from my mother-in-law. A few minutes later, she knocked.

"Excuse me," she said.

"Yes?" I said.

"Why is that ham sitting in my sink?"

"It's soaking."

"Don't you need water for something to soak?"

No! The sink couldn't have drained! Stupid cheap sink! I needed every minute until that ham went into the oven. It had to be the perfect ham.

I soared down the stairs and into the kitchen. This time, I slammed the stopper down hard. I rubbed the ham. A little chunk of slimy fat lodged between my fingers. *Eww,* I thought. No, I corrected myself. Not *eww.* This is how hams are supposed to behave.

"It's going to be okay, baby," I said.

Regina entered the kitchen.

"Are you giving that ham a massage?" she said.

"Yes," I said. "It needs me."

———— ●—

That Christmas, my mother-in-law had finally moved, but we had other problems. An epic ice storm hit Nashville, hemming us all into her town house, which would have been cozy and easily escapable in good weather but now had started to resemble *Cell Block H,* with a toddler. The ham became a point of contention.

"That's too big for my oven," my mother-in-law said.

"No it's not," I said.

"Yes," she said. "It is. I don't have a pot big enough to cook it in."

"We'll figure something out," I said.

"I'm worried that it'll be too salty," she said.

"I'm soaking it," I said. "Don't worry."

"I really don't see how you're going to cook it."

"Listen here," I said. "I bought this ham and I *am* going to cook it!"

"Don't get mad at my mom," Regina said. "She's just trying to help."

Later, under my breath, I said to Regina, "She's not trying to help. She's trying to ruin my ham. I know she doesn't want to eat it. I know that none of you does. But

I'm making this ham and no one is going to stop me. DO YOU UNDERSTAND?"

"Mommy, Daddy," Elijah said. "Pick me up!"

"Just a second, honey," I said. "Daddy has to soak his ham."

That evening, as I continued to massage my ham in its cold-water bath, I accidentally got into a conversation with my mother-in-law about faith. She suspected that there was a secular humanist in her midst. I tried to dodge.

"You don't really practice, do you?" she said.

"Well, um, uh, well, uh, not really, but I still observe the holidays for Elijah, because I think it's, uh, good for him to, um, know traditions and all. We light Hanukkah candles and have Passover dinner."

"Eventually y'all are going to have to make a decision."

"I think that if we raise him knowing about a lot of different faiths, it'll be fine," I said. "I kind of think of it as an education in comparative religion."

By the look on her face, I might as well have told her that I will raise my son to believe that Satan is King.

That night, my son sensed that the golden day was drawing near. I desperately tried to be a good dad on Christmas.

"Santa outside!" he said.

"Soon," I said.

"Elijah see Santa!" he said.

"Santa will come while you're sleeping," I said.

Regina had found a forty-year-old Little Golden Book

edition of *The Night Before Christmas*. I read it to Elijah as a bedtime story, taking time between verses to stop him from drinking a bottle of Nana's Wite-Out. He went to sleep at seven, but at eight we heard him rumbling. I went in.

"Elijah miss Santa Claus," he said.

"No you didn't," I said. "He's not here."

"Elijah want open presents from Santa!"

"Elijah," I said. "You have to go to sleep, or Santa won't bring you any presents. He'll bring them while you're sleeping."

"Waaaaah!" he said. "Santa!"

Regina had taken to bed again with her evil stomach bacteria. I was baking her yearly batch of oatmeal chocolate-chip cookies. I decided I could do anything in the kitchen.

"Daddy's making cookies for Santa," I said.

"Santa eat Daddy cookies!" said Elijah.

"That's right," I said. "Now can you go to sleep like a good boy?"

"Yeah," he said.

So I went downstairs and lovingly mixed up the batter and put it in the oven while my mother-in-law watched *Law and Order* in the next room, petting her ancient, bitter cat, obviously wanting me out of her space. Believe me, I wanted out, too. The cookies got done and they were delicious. I put half a cookie and some crumbs on a plate, and put a little soy milk in a plastic cup, covering it with foil so the cat wouldn't spill it overnight. Then I put the plate and cup by the fireplace.

"So Elijah can see it when he wakes up," I said.

"Isn't that sweet?" my mother-in-law said.

I've never believed in Santa. He wasn't a presence in my childhood. But why shouldn't Elijah? The kid was two, for God's sake. What kind of dad doesn't let his kid believe in Santa Claus?

"Mmm," I said. "These cookies are good."

In the sink, my ham soaked in its seventh change of water.

"Tomorrow," I said, "you're gonna shine."

———— ⬩ ————

The recipe called for me to bake the ham in the oven for three hours plus in a roasting pan, wrapped in foil with four cups of water. Regina did the foil wrapping and the water pouring.

"Shit!" she said.

"What?" I said.

"The water keeps coming out onto the pan. Why didn't you get heavy-duty foil?"

I gritted my teeth.

"Because," I said, "no one told me to."

"Everyone knows you cook ham in heavy-duty foil."

"I don't even know what heavy-duty foil is."

Dinner arrived soon enough. The audience for my ham

included: my mother- and sister-in-law, both of whom eat like rabbits that can't wait to get to the gym; my wife, who had the aforementioned nasty stomach bacteria; my five-year-old nephew, Westlund, and newborn niece, Mackensie (Note: These are not Jewish names); Elijah; my brother-in-law; and me. The ham came out of the oven. Expecting something magnificent, I unfolded the heavy-duty foil that we'd picked up from Walgreens at the eleventh hour. The ham looked slimy and unappealing, like something on a veterinarian's autopsy table. I spent forty-five minutes trimming off just enough fat to make it edible. And then I tried to make red-eye gravy, which just tasted like smoky water. My sister-in-law added extra coffee, and then it tasted like smoky, watery coffee.

The ham was very, very, very, very, very salty. I might as well have rubbed a salt lick in bacon fat and set it on the table.

"This is delicious," said my sister-in-law, as she ate other things.

Regina and I cook all the time, and often with great success. But the ham tasted vile. After dinner, we had thirty pounds of it left. We tried to pawn some of it off on my relatives.

"We don't really eat stuff that's already been cured," Brett said. "So it would be wasted on us."

There are moments when a man sees himself clearly. That was, for me, one of those moments. I felt my heart disintegrate.

It wouldn't do for me to throw ninety percent of my prize ham into the trash, so I started carving off the bone. I carved and carved. My wrists ached worse than after my typical four-hour workday.

"I'm done," I said.

My mother-in-law turned the ham over.

"You've still got half a ham to go," she said.

Regina and I took almost all the ham home with us on the airplane. For two days, it sat in the refrigerator. Then we froze it. One morning, I said, "Let's have ham and eggs."

We got a serving of ham out of the freezer. The fat had coagulated into thick yellow globules. We looked at it, and looked at each other. And I threw the bag into the trash.

"Next year," I said, "we're making lasagne."

RUM BALLS

Roger Director

———◆—◆———

$\mathcal{E}$very Christmas, thousands of wealthy Americans open their houses to some of the country's most ragged, foul-smelling scum—their child's college friends. These are individuals who, if they even got past the security gate would normally have been torn to bits by guard dogs, and yet they must be housed and dined simply because they share a bathroom or a classroom or a sexually transmitted disease with Junior.

If you're the friend being invited, you've spent at least a semester hearing how screwed-up your friend's parents are, and telling your friend how screwed-up yours are, and now you get to see for yourself. What better time than Christmas to watch a family at its most dysfunctional? This is when all Christians torture themselves trying to have a Christmas just like one they never had in the first place. What is that, if not mass delusion?

But this doesn't befall everybody. Some escape. Being Jewish helps.

I didn't know whether or not Penelope Gund was devout about Christmas when I was invited to spend the holiday at her home, but I knew she was the most un-Jewish person I'd met in two years at college.

The reason I was going was simple. I had a car; Penelope was taking her girlfriend Ryan back home for Christmas, and neither had wheels.

Ryan was a vivid freshman from Seattle whom Penelope had encountered at her first Bryn Mawr tea. Penelope was tall and tapered as a carrot and looked out over her granny glasses as if she didn't care about a thing, whereas Ryan counted any day as bad during which for one second she had ceased pursuing her ambition to make an original contribution to mankind. She wanted to create so many new vaccines they'd have to invent new diseases.

I'd had Ryan in my sights since I met her. Now was my chance. I had a car. I would achieve a singular ascent in her esteem by making myself impossible to avoid. Lately, Ryan had been ingeniously evasive. For the past week, she'd begun altering her schedule and her movements—never in her library carrel after dinner; taking the West exit from the dining hall instead of the East—ever since, during a late-night study session for an art history test, I'd said, "If I have to look at any more of these fat, little Jesus babies, I'll stab myself in the head." She looked at me with one of those frowns that said I carelessly just had.

My nineteen-year-old logic dictated that the inability to

avoid me would result in Ryan wanting to have sex. My plan had this working for it: Penelope had said she lived in "a small place" in Tunbridge, Vermont, and I pictured overloaded, haphazard sleeping arrangements that might induce Ryan to get a little less chilly.

Penelope's boyfriend was coming, too. Jim. He was the biggest Christian I'd ever met. Literally. He weighed about 375 pounds. And he was an African from the West Indies. He was about six feet two inches square, with wavy hair that fell down way below his shoulders and an unkempt black goatee. He looked like a giant walking groin. Watching Penelope's parents and four sisters meet Jim was going to be great theater. Ryan and I could only bond over that spectacle.

Penelope's house stood at the end of a long drive between rows of sugar maples. "Small" turned out to be what folks of Penelope's ilk called "a pile"—three stories' worth. There were outbuildings. Real outbuildings. The only building I'd ever been in that started with the word *out* had no plumbing. Penelope's "little" home in Vermont was, in fact, a compound.

James, Ryan, and I stretched and rubbed our arms and squinted at our own frosty breath and gaped at the tree-spired horizon while Penelope rapped on the red front door and glanced down at a heap of her younger sisters' L.L.Bean snow boots.

Mrs. Gund turned out to be a stale-looking smaller version of Penelope. Her eyes rounded with cheer at the sight of her eldest daughter. The four younger sisters floated like sylphs toward the entrance, as if carried on a waft of cinnamon and clove spice and Christmas cookie baking.

In other words, this was the Christmas tableau you'd see spinning around on the metal greeting card carousel at the local pharmacy while you were waiting on line to buy a condom.

"Are you ready for the shit to hit the fan?" I asked James.

"For what?" James said. He was drawing a blank. Which is why I loved James so much. No matter his appearance, he walked with innocence.

Mrs. Gund had never greeted anyone at her red front door who was wearing a dashiki, not to mention one the size of a termite tarp. Maybe that's why she held out her hand to me and said, "I've heard so much about you, James."

"Mother, *this* is James," Penelope quickly corrected, redirecting her mother's attention.

"It's a pleasure to meet you, Mrs. Gund," James said, like the proper Groton grad he was.

Mrs. Gund was soon back in the kitchen looking even staler than before, marinating her holiday specialty—bunny rabbit. Hopping had always been a disqualifier for me when I got to noodling the merits of food I loved. But this was Christmas. Mrs. Gund was also rolling out "rum balls" according to the recipe of an old aunt Audrey in Auburn, Alabama.

Meanwhile, James engaged the sisters, Avery, Anthea, Sally, and Jen. When he sat, his thighs became park benches. They took turns. Ten-year-old Avery perched on James's vast lap, and he joked, "What do you want for Christmas, little girl?" and we all laughed because he was the perfect Santa.

Penelope's father, Errol, was away at "the kingdom," which, Penelope explained, was a swatch of hillside ten miles away where he intended to build a new Valhalla.

"Everyone's got to see 'the kingdom,'" she said. "Dad stands there and takes a deep breath and looks out. 'Nothing but splendor. Far as the eye can see,' he says." Penelope used her dad's deep voice and imitated the majestic wave of his arm.

Since retiring from the State Department, Errol Gund spent most of his time at "the kingdom." Even though (as I instantly saw after, when we emerged from the woods) there was nothing there. At least, nothing visible to maintain. There was just Mr. Gund standing at the northwest corner of a stony, fifty-acre meadow that faced the Connecticut River Valley. Mr. Gund had a barrel chest and a chalky face and a noticeable overbite. He held a coffee mug, but the twist he gave his mouth every time he took a sip seemed to say he was experiencing something other than caffeine. A series of unfinished wood pegs were driven into the ground near his feet. Slender red string wound around them.

Errol Gund was standing in what would one day be his living room when Mrs. Gund said, "This is James." Mr. Gund blinked and looked down at his pegs.

"Welcome to the kingdom, James," Mr. Gund said.

"Thank you, Mr. Gund. It's quite beautiful," James said like the proper doctor's son he was.

Everyone thought it was beautiful. Ryan shouted, "Merry Christmas!" and bounded downhill into the wind, in a gleeful, free-spirited gambol. She glanced over her shoulder, straight back at me. I realized maybe she expected me to take off with her, to gambol downhill alongside in ecstatic, liberated communion.

I didn't. I wasn't much of a gamboler.

Before dinner, Mr. Gund lifted his glass and, from memory, chanted in Old English what he said was a thousand-year-old wassail toast, something straight out of *Beowulf*:

"Wealhoeo malpelode, heo fore paem werede spraec . . ."

After rabbit stew, we sat by the fire, Penelope's father in a pale yellow, button-down Brooks Brothers shirt and tan cuffed pants. He'd brought his glass from the table. And a tray of Mrs. Gund's special holiday rum balls.

I tried one of them. Mainly out of politeness. I gagged. It was all I could do to keep the eyeballs in my head. On my list of favorite spherical foods, they'd go way below matzah balls and meatballs. Mr. Gund popped them like Raisinets.

Two white sofas flanked the mantel, from which Christmas stockings hung. Mr. Gund and James sat opposite each other. Penelope involved herself in prodding and poking the logs. Her mother sat at the end of the couch closest to her. Mrs. Gund clasped some creased, stained song sheets for carols she intended for us all to sing. "I'm so happy you made it home for Christmas," she told Penelope with tears in her eyes.

Ryan examined the Christmas tree, taken right off the kingdom's own land. Ryan admired the ornaments, old and handmade.

"We have one back home in Seattle. It's this hollowed-out sort of giant acorn with the Magi in it. It's been in my mother's family for generations. It was on her mother's tree. It was on her grandmother's tree. And it was on her great-grandmother's tree."

"There's something about a beautiful old ornament like that," I said, realizing I had no idea, yet hoping I didn't sound too much that way. But Ryan didn't seem to mind. She was warming to me. She liked telling me about her old Christmas tree ornaments. We paused to appreciate the crackling fire.

"Did you see him this afternoon at 'the kingdom'?" I whispered to Ryan.

"Who?"

"Mr. Gund."

"What about him?"

"When he saw James he looked like he wanted to yank those stakes from the ground," I said.

I was trying to sound familiar, but Ryan looked put off. "Don't you see, James is his *worst nightmare*," I said.

"You're so immature," Ryan said, and she moved away.

Mr. Gund slapped his knees, rose, and showed us some of the things he had amassed in embassies overseas. He finished off a couple more rum balls, then took a carved wooden African mask down from the wall and let his hands play along its smooth finish and knobby cheeks. This was a special tribal mask, he said. He explained that it was a fertility god, and it had been presented to him as a gift for helping out in a disagreement between one tribe and an adversary who threatened to consume their livers if not given enough sacred parrot feathers.

"Mind if I examine that, sir?" James asked.

"Be my guest," Mr. Gund said, handing over the mask and, on the way back to his seat, dispatching the remaining rum balls. Mr. Gund's face was beginning to look red. Beads of perspiration appeared along his forehead. You could see how his hair was thinning, because the redder he got, the more his scalp shined through.

Avery came over. She sat on James's knee and looked at the mask as if for the first time. Her sudden, intense interest seemed to prompt James. He saw how intrigued she was. He lifted the mask and put it over his face and playfully growled, "Tell me what you want for Christmas, little girl," for maybe the twentieth time, which never failed to crack them both up.

Mr. Gund looked distracted. He muttered something and retired to the bedroom. Mrs. Gund said, "I guess we'll sing these tomorrow," and then told everyone where to find the bedroom they'd been assigned. This organizational chore seemed to brighten her increasingly pale cheeks.

James snored. Nothing could sound so loud. The flight deck of an aircraft carrier in full battle operation, maybe. My bones rattled from the sonic waves.

I hadn't wound up bunking anywhere near Ryan. Mrs. Gund had secured her and the other girls in their own wing and sentenced me to bunking in the same room as James. I thought to myself abjectly, "Some Christmas Eve this is," before remembering I didn't celebrate the holiday.

I tried every mental trick I knew to get to sleep. Counting was no good. I imagined I was homeless, sleeping on a street grate on a frigid night in the dead of winter—a sort of reverse-psychological ploy to relish what comfort I had. But that didn't work.

I decided not to recoil from James's snoring, but to welcome it, accept it, treat it like part of the environment. I mentally catalogued his fascinating assortment of snores. A series of harsh, booming exhales, sort of like surfacing whales clearing their blowholes. Punctuated by raspy bleats like a bugler's call to charge. Then a long, excruciating tearing wail that sounded like a torso being fed through a mill saw.

Nothing worked. I laughed to myself. James, the Santa, snoring next to me, dead to the world, while he ought to be off on his sleigh like a whirlwind.

The inability to sleep inevitably focuses your mind on one of the most profound questions of human existence: "What am I doing here?" That's what I asked myself finally, in the dark of that Christmas Eve. "What am I doing here? In this house? For Christmas? Chasing a girl who looks at me as if I were a bowl of soggy corn flakes? What am I doing here?"

My last resort was to combat noise with noise itself. There was a turntable on the nightstand beside my bed. A pair of headphones was plugged into it. I snagged them from the floor and snapped them over my ears. For a moment, there was silence. But the headphones proved no barrier to James. I could have predicted that. Now I turned on the phonograph. The record spun. I dropped the arm at the end of the album in the smooth, black, grooveless inner ring where the needle could glide and drift endlessly, like a raft bobbing on the waves. A gentle, sensuous tropical wind spilled out of the headphones and into my brain. I turned up the volume. My head bobbed back onto the pillow.

Shhhhhhhssssssssssshhhhhhhhhhhhhhh. Shhhhhhhssssss-ssssshhhhhhhhhhhh.

I was asleep in seconds.

ONLY TO BE WOKEN UP BY A TERRIBLE NOISE. Errol Gund was standing in the doorway screaming and waving a gun. He's here to shoot James, I thought.

I couldn't hear distinctly what Mr. Gund was saying. I jacked myself up on my elbows, blinking and realizing there was something on my head—oh, the headphones. I tugged them off and immediately heard the deafening roar of accumulating hell blasting from the phonograph speakers out into the room and the rest of the house.

"TALK ABOUT THE MIDNIGHT RAMBLER . . ."

At that moment, Mr. Gund's revolver muzzle spat red. The phonograph exploded in pieces.

That stopped the music. Mr. Gund lurked for a moment in the half-dark of the hallway before he turned away to address approaching expressions of alarm from upstairs.

My heart was pounding. My ears felt wronged. I saw that my headphones were no longer connected to the phonograph. That might explain why the music had begun blasting from the record player speakers. I must have rolled over and yanked the headphones out . . . and the needle must have automatically begun playing the record again. What album was it? "Midnight Rambler" was on *Let It Bleed*. Or was it *Beggars Banquet*?

None of this woke James. He continued snoring. He was oblivious. And then I realized: Mr. Gund hadn't come downstairs in a rum ball–fueled rage to silence his daughter's freakish boyfriend and take a potshot at Satan's version of a potential son-in-law. He'd been enraged by *me*.

I got out of bed and snuck a look. The sisters and Ryan were arrayed along the landing in their nightclothes sniffing

at the greasy cloud of gunpowder that overcame the scent
of baked sugar from the kitchen.

"I heard an intruder, all right?" Mr. Gund was telling
them in a gruff voice that sounded more irritated than reas-
suring. He had already laid the gun aside on a table among
some pocket change and mail, as if hoping it might be cam-
ouflaged in the scatter. He tried to move things along. "Nobody's hurt. Go back to sleep."

Aunt Audrey's rum balls can do that to you.

———— • ————

The next morning there was a pot of coffee on the kitchen
counter. Some mugs had been put out. Also a pint of
mocha-flavored creamer and a small wicker basket holding
a blue-and-pink rank of sugar packets. People moved about
in hushed tones, but I couldn't tell if it was any more quiet
than usual.

Then Penelope's mother said, "That certainly gave me a
fright last night." She held a cup of coffee between her hands
and looked down and away, her eyes wistful and sorrowful.

"What happened, Mrs. Gund?" James said. He hadn't
seen anyone yet. He was returning from a run, wearing a
boysenberry-colored sweat suit. He had knotted a yellow
bandanna around his forehead. He looked like a costumed
advertisement for some store or another, the kind you see
holding an arrow and telling people to come in and pick up
a bargain.

"I woke up to go running and I saw the record player was all . . ." James went, "Pssssh." A mini-explosion. Then he laughed. And all the girls laughed.

"You slept through it," I told him.

"Slept through what?" James said, and everyone howled. Mrs. Gund, Penelope, all her sisters, and Ryan. Absolutely howled, all the more because James didn't get why they were laughing.

"Mr. Gund took a shot at me last night," I said for James's benefit. He looked really puzzled and seemed to be owed an explanation of some sort about the sudden raucous laughter.

"No kidding?" James said.

"But he missed," said Mrs. Gund, making a joke. She had evidently gained a better mood. There were carols playing on the radio. All eyes turned to the Christmas tree and the mounds of colorfully wrapped gifts beneath it.

"Your father's already left for 'the kingdom,'" Mrs. Gund said. She seemed pleased that he was gone. "Let's open the presents now."

The Gund sisters bolted for the tree. Ryan beamed at the sight. I beamed, too. I felt comforted, as if watching a calamity from a safe distance. But I knew I'd never understand these people.

BUY HUMBUG

Cintra Wilson

———◆———

*I*t's Holiday time again, and it's the most wonderful time of year if you're an upper-middle-class Methodist mom in the middle of the country, living in a sprawling, ranch-style house that glows like a jewel box in the snowy landscape and just screams "cozy." Your glamorous and intelligent children are rushing home for the holidays in colorful woolens from their universities back East. Everyone is looking forward to singing carols in the original German around the grand piano and arguing about poetry and legal torts around the grand ol' fir tree. Whole haunches of aged Angus are dragged out of the garage livestock refrigerator along with ducks that Dad shot, and hams are fruitily decorated to look like Pucci dartboards. The scent of fragrant pine blends with the salivary aromas of sugar, pork, clove, and burning butter. Affluent and witty neighbors stroll by drawing an old sled to drop off large steaming pies and expensive gifts wrapped in metallic paper.

Great-grand-nonny's real silver lies on the table next to the Wedgwood gravy boat and the whimsical party crackers imported from England. Elaborate wreaths of holly surround thick scented candles above the roaring fireplace. There are a few well-behaved and precocious three- and four-year-olds who scamper about in little plush footie suits and say stunningly hilarious things about "Tanta Coz tumming dowd the chimby!" Their innocent joy is palpable and infectious.

Then there's everyone else: the vast majority of less-fortunate people in the world who fucking dread the holidays. They spend Xmas in their lousy apartments lighting cigarettes off the space heater, unshaven and sniveling, wearing the clothes they slept in, drinking vodka straight out of the plastic-handle jug, and watching the burning Yule Log on TV until it actually seems to have dialogue.

Holiday cheer is scarce for the lonely, broke, and downtrodden. The only reindeer those people are likely to encounter is the one on the front of the Jagermeister bottle. The aggressively cheerful facade of the holiday season holds nothing for the desperate, and tacitly implies that the disheveled sad sack has failed by not creating an idyllic and luxurious family situation for himself, if for no other reason than the sake of hosting this annual holiday virus.

Many people are forced to stave off severe seasonal depression by such jarring stimuli as big-death action movies. It is no coincidence that many of the biggest-budget, Schwarzenegger-genre, shoot-'em-in-the-face films open on Xmas Day. Watching wrathful murders makes depressed people feel strong. They walk home in the cold to their empty apartments, hopped up on the sexy pump of rage, hoping some reasonable-size asshole will say something obnoxious to them so they can feel justified in kicking him until he doesn't move anymore.

"Howdya like that, heh?" One fantasizes leering as the sorry perp squirms in the gutter. "Merry F-ing Christmas."

This violent escapism is certainly less painful than staying home and watching *It's a Wonderful Life* and crying hot, piteous tears for yourself when everything turns out to be OK at the end. "When will I get my happy ending?" you sob between pizza nuggets. Not this Xmas.

Those in the lower to middle class who suffer suburban holidays endure a whole other variety of torture, primarily in the form of needless family strain. There is an unwritten law, probably espoused by the airline industry, that long-distance families, even those who don't really like each other, are supposed to fork over vast sums to travel to be together for the winter holidays.

The airlines, writhing flirtily with profit, really go all the way with their holiday spirit and usually show as their in-flight "entertainment" some vomitously cloying Xmas propaganda porn flick with a title like *The Greatest Gift Ever*, wherein a high-school student has a kidney removed to save his beloved great-aunt, Debbie Reynolds; everyone recovers in time to sing "Silent Night" and cry with deep familial joy.

Once one finally gets home, one is forced to embrace soused, embarrassing relatives with handlebar moustaches whom one would rather never see again, and laugh indulgently when unwrapping such appalling and worthless gift items as rainbow-toe socks and electric tongue-scrapers. Yuletide food is usually a throwback to the days of frenzied pagan gluttony and the Satanic zeal that cookbooks in the 1950s had for the excessive uses of starch, shortening, and meat drippings. Since ninety-eight percent of the women in America hate their bodies too much to tolerate having flesh on them, the holidays are a time of either painful abstinence or outright self-loathing.

———◆—

Xmas today is a feverish, mindless, and unregenerate overspending orgy. It is the Great Guilt Trip, the buy-a-little-something-for-everyone-you-love disease that corporate America has infected our lives with, via the Trojan horse of a "religious holiday." To personify and encourage this lemming-like leap into massive consumer debt, we have our charming, portly mascot Saint Nick. I discovered after perusing Butler's indispensable classic, *Lives of the Saints,* that Saint Nicholas's biography has suffered horribly from telephone-style bastardization. Saint Nicholas of Myra was a pious young man in fourth-century Asia Minor who came into money following the death of his well-off parents. Upon hearing of a local man who had plans to sell his three daughters into prostitution, Nicholas threw a small sack of money through the man's window, providing the oldest girl with a dowry and thus enabling her to marry. As the other two girls came of age, he performed the same charitable act to offset their future whoredom. As a result, Saint Nicholas was represented in visual folklore as someone who tossed small sacks around. Due to the crude artistic renderings of these sacks, many early Christians mistook the sacks for children's heads, giving rise to the rumor that Saint Nick had rescued and revived three children who had been slain by an evil innkeeper and subsequently pickled in a brine tub. Thus, Saint Nicholas became the patron saint of children. In short, the true legend of Saint Nicholas is a damned far cry from a fat, bearded yutz from the North Pole who slides down the chimney and brings Barbies and Hot Wheels to all the children of the world. If you're considering selling your children into prostitution, perhaps you'll get a visit from Saint Nick. Taken into actual historical context, the whole charade of going to Macy's to let one's children climb into the lap of a drunk who looks like he's been upholstered by Italian pimps in order for them to bark out their greedy consumer object lust is bogus and unwarranted, and the chilling result of corporate brainwashing.

***

There are positive aspects of Xmas that people tend to dwell on when struggling to achieve the "holiday spirit." Xmas is the only time of year when senior citizens get dragged out of whatever urine-cave they are inhabiting and are allowed to mingle with the general population. There are lots of parties, which enables lonely single people to raid their friends' medicine cabinets for Vicodin.

And there is that moment sometimes, when a transcendent hush falls over the dark street, and there is some unnameable thrill in the icy air, a collective human exuberance, and one looks at the tiny blinking stars through the spidery fingers of naked trees and feels full of a weird and wild hope.

***

But I usually miss that moment because I'm pouring boiling water all over some child's snowman. I've compiled a list of other holiday activities to offset Yuletide misanthropy:

1. Make a big gingerbread crack house tenement with boarded-up windows and frosting graffiti all over it,

and have Playmobil characters inside smoking little glass pipes filled with powdered sugar.

2. Make a sad snowman who is sitting down on the sidewalk, then put a crudely written cardboard sign next to it that says, I AM A 56 YEAR OLD VIETNAM VETERIN [SIC] WITH HEPOTITIS C PLEASE HELP. Make sure you put out an old hat, and come by every half hour or so to collect the money for your very own Christmas drug fund.

3. Here's a real Xmas-morning "stumper": Instead of toys in the stocking for the young ones around the house, fill each stocking on the hearth with a prosthetic foot. A real ampu-teaser.

4. Find any church nativity scene and surround it with POLICE LINE—DO NOT CROSS tape, then make it look like Baby Jesus shot one of the three kings with a handgun. Optional: Jesus can have a talk balloon saying, "I thought the frankincense was a gun!"

A two-headed baby Jesus is also a fun changeling substitution.

Another fun one is to rip up cotton balls and throw ketchup on them, in front of the fireplace. That way, when everyone comes into the living room for Xmas morning, you can say, "Uh-oh. White hair and blood. Looks like the dog got him. Poor Santa."

The important thing to remember is that "festivity" is relative. No matter who you are, you deserve to have a happy holiday, and you should make sure you get one *by any means necessary.*

In excelsis, by Deo.

THE GIFT THAT DID NOT NEED WRAPPING

Elizabeth Noble

———◆———

I'd have a nerve claiming that any of my thirty-seven Christmases has been other than pretty close to idyllic. I was your average middle-class kid. I've had some crackers. (Ha, ha, crackers!) I think I remember the year—it must have been 1973—when my dad and my grandfather went to the pub for a few (too many) pints on Christmas Eve, and then had to build the wooden toy shop my mum had hidden in the back of the car. It took four hours, apparently. And when we woke up, my sister and I thought Father Christmas had bought us a dog kennel (for the dog we didn't have).

Nineteen eighty-three was the year Father Christmas very kindly bought me the earrings that would fit the pierced ears my mother had told me I was too young to get—I guess he persuaded her otherwise, clever old guy.

It was 1994 when my now husband bought me the perfect silver necklace that let me know he was (a) interested, and (b) tasteful (phew).

The best one so far (see, a Christmas optimist) was 1997, when my first child was a few weeks old and we "wrapped" her in colorful things and lay her gently under the tree, to take the first twenty of the twenty thousand Christmas photographs we now have of her.

But there was this one year . . .

You first need to understand that my mother is a Christmas nutter. We're talking Christmas-o-rama in every room. In the 1980s there were definitely multicolored glitter-ball things stuck to the living room ceiling with Blu Tack. There were salt dough choirboys teetering back and forth on sideboards (also requiring Blu Tack). Every year we had a two-foot-tall cardboard Santa, which my mum made, with a cotton wool beard and rather flat cardboard arms secured with those brass pins that splay out; he lived next to the television (the one that always showed *The Wizard of Oz* and *The Sound of Music*). It was a really big deal. My older sister has inherited the rogue gene that allows you to believe that erecting a large polythene Santa-with-sack on the side of your house in late November is acceptable behavior. I, myself, did not escape completely, although I like to think of myself as altogether more stylish. More Shaker, less Bollywood. I start making my lists in October. What to buy. What to cook. What to wear.

Since I married eight years ago, I have had to eradicate

all my husband's own familial Christmas habits. Opening presents in pajamas. Eating red cabbage flavored with cinnamon. Stockings in the bedrooms. That all had to go. When it comes to Christmas, I'm a "my way or the highway" kind of a girl.

My brother once saw Santa Claus. He was certain he'd seen him in his room one year. He continued to believe this until he was quite old. I'm not actually sure he still doesn't, and that he might just have said he didn't to avoid being beaten up. I don't know how he copes now; he married a Dutch girl, and has to do the whole thing at the beginning of December, with entirely different foodstuffs.

It's not our fault, this slight seasonal dolallyness. It's a hereditary condition. My grandmother was the original sinner. My mother (a real war baby, born at Christmas in 1940, after my grandfather had gone to fight with General Montgomery and the Desert Rats in Africa) grew up in a village called Sixpenny Handley (yes, really), in Dorset, in a kind of postwar austerity, which meant that they never had any money (or ever saw bananas, which is a weird thought). But sure enough, each year my grandmother would go into epic debt with this mythical character, the tally man (who, in my childish imagination, always looked a little like the Child Catcher in *Chitty Chitty Bang Bang,* but who was very probably a quite ordinary bloke making a living, albeit off the dangerous dreams of the poor), in order to buy each of her children their one new outfit a year, and the gifts that she would spend the next eleven months paying off. My mother and her brothers were sent to the market late on Christmas Eve to buy cut-price clementines. If you think this is sounding a little Dickens, I totally agree. You can hear the poignant violin and the scratching of Tiny Tim's crutch now, can't you? But I think rural England in the late 1940s and early 1950s was a bit like that if you were working class, which they were. Once on a family holiday, we went to a pioneer village, the kind where all the staff dresses in crinoline. My mum and dad spent the whole time saying, "We had one of these," and "This is how we used to do the washing/light fires/iron clothes." It was mortifying.

We did the same thing every year. Come mid-December, my mum dressed the fake tree, which, at least, was green—we knew someone once who had an electric pink one, to match her living room (scary)—and the rest of the house to within an inch of its life. My birthday is the twenty-second of December, a real source of contention. With my mum being a late-December baby herself, I grew up thinking that my parents had been grossly irresponsible the previous March. It did not help when my mother told me I had been conceived—very deliberately—on Mothering Sunday, what to Americans is known as Mother's Day. My birthday was the day my grandparents would arrive. They watched a lot of television, as I remember. On Christmas morning, my father would go down to make tea and "check" that Father Christmas had come, and then we would all have to wash and dress, to a rousing soundtrack of high-pitched choir-boys squeaking carols, before we were allowed to file downstairs in order of age (very von Trapp). Christmas lunch was served after the Queen's Speech, and that, too, was always exactly the same. Same flavoring in the gravy, same vegetables, nothing mucked about with: no slivers of almonds in among our Brussels sprouts, and absolutely no maple glaze on our roast parsnips, thank you very much. And brandy butter, not sauce, and not made with brown sugar or vanilla sugar or anything other than white icing sugar and unsalted butter. Oh, and thick, viscous egg nog on Christmas Eve. Which was just exactly how we all liked it, once every three hundred and sixty-five days.

My point is this: Mum created this incredible, ritualistic, comfort blanket of a Christmas, which, approaching adolescence, I was deeply rude about but, secretly, completely addicted to.

In fact, approaching adolescence, I was deeply rude about pretty much everything. I was sort of angry about everything, too. When I was eleven, we moved from England to Toronto, Canada. Blue skies and snow at Christmas, after years of gray, damp, inclement weather. But, nevertheless, uprooted without consultation, I found the whole thing the most wonderful opportunity to be both angry and rude, on a large scale. I'd been happy where I was, and I was damned if I was going to be happy there. I'd show them. They'd jolly well think twice before giving me opportunities they'd never dreamt of and an exciting, adventurous life in a staggeringly beautiful country ever again. Oh yes.

Actually, I don't know how they didn't kill me. I threw a serious strop about having to go to the Rockies, when all my friends were going to Florida. "Some people like mountains, and some people don't." And some people should probably have been sent home immediately to some Dotheboys Hall–style detention center for the terminally ungrateful.

I was ever so plain as a teenager. My mouse-brown hair clung greasily and lifelessly to my head. My teeth protruded—a long way. I've got the kind of face that frankly is never going to win prizes but looks a hell of a lot better when it's smiling and happy—I can sometimes, on a really good day, almost sparkle. But there wasn't a lot of that going on. Add to that the fact that I didn't speak properly— how I hated my English accent—or dress properly (I remember wanting a Lacoste T-shirt, Jordache jeans, and a LeSportsac handbag more than life itself), wasn't Jewish (long story—it was a very Jewish neighborhood, and I wanted Hebrew lessons and a Bat Mitzvah), and couldn't get a volleyball back over the net if it was thrown to me from three feet away—those things bruise.

At least I'd have Christmas, hey?

Apparently not. We were going to spend Christmas Day at the home of friends. Huh! "Friends" wouldn't want to mess up your English Christmas. It was bad enough that we'd had to go out into the state, eat donuts, and drink hot chocolate, then wade through snow and chop down our own flipping Christmas tree. What was wrong with the fake one? But, no. Yet again, my parents had taken a major family decision without consultation. One of Mum and Dad's friends ran the Opera Company in Toronto, and he was planning a major celebration at his home for all the touring waifs and strays who couldn't get home for the holidays. And for us, who could have stayed at home.

We were not happy, my brother and sister and I. We moaned and railed. We extracted a promise from Mum that we could have a "proper" Christmas Day on Boxing Day. With the right routine and the right food. And then grudgingly agreed to go. Mum made a huge crepe-paper Christmas cracker to take (it took two people to hold it), with a small gift for everyone inside, but we were not so cheaply bought.

The day started badly when I opened my Christmas present. Sitting in a tiny box under the Christmas tree, it did not look like either designer gear, a voucher for braces, or a copy of the Torah, so expectation was not running high. It was a gold-plated travel alarm clock, engraved with my name and the date. Oh dear. I'd like to say I won an Oscar for my performance as grateful teenager. But you wouldn't believe me, would you, and you'd be right. This Christmas was not going well.

I must admit the people were interesting. European, Middle Eastern, North American. Singers, makeup artists, directors. All theatrically expansive, warm, engaging. I had never been around people like that before, and it was exciting. And I'd have been quite happy if I'd been watching them from afar, undetected. But they were being nice to me, trying to talk to me. I'd never felt so out of place, and so uninteresting, and so far away from being the kind of grown-up that they were, that I wanted to be. I was miserable and wretched, and I just wanted to leave.

At lunch I was seated near a set designer. I remember him exactly—how he looked, how he was dressed. But I don't remember the lunch. I still have a framed drawing of the set he designed for *La Belle Helene.*

His name was Thierry. He smiled at my sister. (Here you should know that my sister was born blond, with round curls and big blue eyes and peachy skin. When I followed sixteen months later, scrawny, with spots and straggly black hair, people apparently used to approach my mother on the street, cluck, and smile at my beautiful sister, seated majestically on the seat attached to my mother's big Mary Poppins pram, then peer in at me and find themselves curiously at a loss for words. This, I feel, may have done damage.) Then he said to my sister, in his exotic, enchanting French accent, "I look at you, and I am reminded of a Gainsborough painting." Now, I'm not so sure that either my sister or I knew our Gainsborough from our Jackson Pollock at this point, but we both knew, from his tone and the look in his eyes, that this was good. Very good.

My heart sank. Well, that figured. Could this day stink any more?

Thierry turned to me. I thought again of the pram. What would he manage to come up with? Surely he'd manage something. He practically made a living out of telling women who weighed twenty stone that they made convincing romantic sylphlike heroines, didn't he? I remember holding my breath.

"But you . . ." BUT! Where was he going with this? "But you, you remind me of a woman with whom I was once very much in love."

And so delivered pretty much the best Christmas present that I ever got.

Postscript: The utter selfishness of my parents has continued, I'm sad to report, since those days. Next thing they did was move to Australia, which meant several Christmas Days spent at vast barbecues, eating with twenty or thirty people on long trestles tables besides the pool, under the blazing sun. Dreadful. And now they've "downsized" (read: made their children take back all the textbooks, old school photographs, collection of dolls-around-the-world that had hitherto happily lived at the old family seat) to a flat that, collectively, we do not fit into; now they seem to think it's the turn of their children to provide Christmas for them. This year, they didn't even have a tree. "So much nicer, isn't it, darling, to be in your own home, once you've got children?" Frankly, no, it isn't. What is the sight of your children's incredulous faces, as they sit beneath your magical tree (do you know it's a real one, and we chopped it down ourselves?) opening treasured gifts, compared with Christmas dinner cooked correctly by your own mother?

ABOUT THE CONTRIBUTORS

Writer and performer MIKE ALBO prefers that thinner, Atkins Diet version of Santa who appears in European imagery. His second novel, *The Underminer: The Best Friend Who Casually Destroys Your Life* (written with his longtime pal Virginia Heffernan), comes out in paperback in spring 2006. Check out his website: www.mikealbo.com.

LOUIS BAYARD finds Christmas the ideal occasion for pondering the sodden wreckage of his past and for repeatedly viewing the Marlo Thomas remake of *It's a Wonderful Life*, which he considers to be shamefully undervalued. His most recent novel, *Mr. Timothy*, was a *New York Times* Notable Book. His next novel, *The Pale Blue Eye*, is due out in March 2006.

STANLEY BING is the author of *Sun Tzu Was a Sissy: Conquer Your Enemies, Promote Your Friends, and Wage the Real Art of War; Throwing the Elephant: Zen and the Art of Managing Up;* and *What Would Machiavelli Do? The Ends*

Justify the Meanness, and he reports on corporate life twice monthly in *Fortune* magazine. He is a veteran of many corporate holiday parties and is proud of the fact that he has not disgraced himself at one since Christmas 2002, when he didn't eat enough hors d'oeuvres to offset the effects of that last tumbler of Glenlivet.

ROGER DIRECTOR is a writer-producer living in Santa Monica. His first novel was *A Place to Fall.* He is at work on a new book. And the most beautiful Christmas he ever had was on the beach in Hawaii, watching the hula to "White Christmas."

Come Christmastime, VALERIE FRANKEL works part-time for Santa, designing matching bra-and-panty gift sets that are always a hit with the ladies. Her ninth novel, *Hex and the Single Girl,* comes out in March 2006.

ANNE GIARDINI doesn't like to complain, but she hasn't received a memorable Christmas present since she was ten years old. Her novel *The Sad Truth About Happiness* was published by HarperCollins in the spring of 2005. She is working on another novel, *Nicolo Piccolo,* when she is not practicing law and the violin in Vancouver.

CYNTHIA KAPLAN is the author of several books, only one of which, *Why I'm Like This: True Stories* (Morrow, 2002), has been written and published. Her work has appeared in many newspapers, magazines, journals, and anthologies, and she is the co-writer of the film *Pipe Dream*. Kaplan is also an actress and comedian and performs in the infamous *What I Like About Jew* Christmas shows at the Knitting Factory, in New York City. Her second book is due out soon, or so they say.

MARIAN KEYES spends Christmas worrying that seasonal high winds might take hold of Rudy, her splendid, life-size illuminated reindeer—the envy of the neighborhood—and whisk him off her roof and into someone else's garden. Her new novel, *Anybody Out There?*, will be published in summer 2006.

BINNIE KIRSHENBAUM no longer kicks over the Christmas tree intentionally; the last three times were accidents. Her most recent novel, *An Almost Perfect Moment* (Ecco/HarperCollins), is out in a paperback edition.

JOHN MARCHESE is the author of *Renovations: A Father and Son Rebuild a House and Rediscover Each Other*, and is at work on a book about violin making. Since beginning his writing career with the *Lubbock* [Texas] *Avalanche-Journal*, he has written for dozens of newspapers and magazines. Though he lives in New York, he spends more time in Texas than is good for him.

CATHERINE NEWMAN is the author of the award-winning memoir *Waiting for Birdy: A Year of Frantic Tedium, Neurotic Angst, and the Wild Magic of Growing a Family* (Penguin, 2005) and of the child-raising journal *Bringing Up Ben & Birdy* at BabyCenter.com. She is a contributing editor for *FamilyFun* magazine, and her work has been published in numerous magazines and anthologies, including in the *New York Times* bestseller *The Bitch in the House* (HarperCollins, 2002) and *Toddler* (Seal Press, 2003). She braves the holidays in snowy, hot-cidery, hack-down-your-own-tree-and-love-it Massachusetts.

ELIZABETH NOBLE no longer has time to bitch about having a Christmas birthday (which was how she spent her first thirty Christmas Days). She's too old, and too busy recreating the magic she remembers from her own mother's home for her two daughters, Tallulah and Ottilie, who make believing believable. She's the author of *The Reading Group*. Her next novel, *The Friendship Test*, is due out in January 2006.

ANN PATCHETT has never put up a Christmas tree and immediately regifts all the ornaments she receives. Her latest book is *Truth & Beauty*.

NEAL POLLACK, a Bar Mitzvahed son of Abraham, spends his Christmas pretending to enjoy Christmas with his

Protestant family-in-law. His memoir, *Daddy Was a Sinner,* will be published in the fall of 2006.

Successfully deprogrammed parochial-school survivor JONI RODGERS practices a self-important woo-woo religion called Jewbuddhistianity but still finds herself craving Tater Tot Hotdish and other exotic Protestant comestibles during Advent. Her fifth book, *The Secret Sisters,* comes out in spring 2006. For more on all that, visit www.jonirodgers.com.

AMY KROUSE ROSENTHA is the author of *Encycopedia of an Ordinary ife* and of severa chidren's books. She ives in Chicago. This concludes the worst "no L" joke ever.

MITCHELL SYMONS is a Brit who likes Americans—yup, he's the one—except when they invite him to spend Christmas with them. His latest book is *This Book of More Perfectly Useless Information,* and in the absence of anyone else doing so, he thoroughly recommends it.

CINTRA WILSON likes to spend Christmas Day going from friend's house to friend's house just enjoying all the colorful pills in their medicine cabinets. The paperback of her latest book, *Colors Insulting to Nature,* was released in June 2005. She is currently at work on a novel purely devoted to the spirit of Christmas, entitled *The Yule-Log Archipelago.*